Revised Edition

MEET YOUR MOTHER

A BRIEF INTRODUCTION TO MARY

MEET
YOUR
MOTHER

A BRIEF INTRODUCTION TO MARY

DR. MARK MIRAVALLE

Foreword by
Fr. Michael Gaitley, MIC

LIGHTHOUSE CATHOLIC MEDIA + MARIAN PRESS
2014

Available from either of the following:

Lighthouse Catholic Media, NFP
303 E. State Street
Sycamore, IL 60178

Phone: 866-767-3155
www.lighthousecatholicmedia.org

Marian Helpers Center
Stockbridge, MA 01263

Prayerline: 800-804-3823
Orderline: 800-462-7426
www.marian.org

ISBN: 978-1-59614-306-7

Cover Design: Devin Schadt

Page Layout: Curtis Bohner

Editing and Proofreading: Fr. Michael Gaitley, MIC, David Came,
Andrew Leeco, and Chris Sparks.

Imprimi Potest:
Very Rev. Kazimierz Chwalek, MIC
Provincial Superior
The Blessed Virgin Mary, Mother of Mercy Province
Congregation of Marian Fathers of the Immaculate Conception of the B.V.M.
March 25, 2014

Printed in the United States of America

An earlier edition of this book was published under the title *Meet Your Mother: Or Love Her More*. This revised edition, which is co-published by Lighthouse Catholic Media and Marian Press, now includes a new foreword and conclusion as well as an appendix on Marian consecration. Also, for this revised edition, the original manuscript underwent thorough and extensive editorial work for a much smoother reading experience. Because Lighthouse Catholic Media and Marian Press have a policy of not publishing ongoing private revelation, two chapters have been omitted from the earlier edition.

Contents

Foreword
'Behold, Your Mother' 7

Chapter 1
The Whole Truth About Mary 11

Chapter 2
A Creature Gives Birth to Her Creator? 15

Chapter 3
The 'Perpetual' Virgin 21

Chapter 4
The 'Immaculate' Conception. 29

Chapter 5
Did Mary Die? 37

Chapter 6
Our Spiritual Mother 43

Chapter 7
Is Mary a 'Co-redeemer'? 47

Chapter 8
Who Mediated the Mediator? 57

Chapter 9
'Did You Call Mary a Lawyer?' 65

Chapter 10
A 'New Marian Dogma' in World News? 71

Chapter 11
'Why Is Mary Appearing All Over the Place?'. . . . 83

Chapter 12
'All Who Wear It Will Receive Great Graces' 89

Chapter 13
Our Lady of Lourdes 95

Chapter 14
'In the End, My Immaculate Heart Will Triumph'. . 101

Conclusion
Drawing Closer to a Mother's Love 113

Appendix 1
How To Pray the Rosary 119

Appendix 2
Introduction to Marian Consecration. 125

Endnotes 131

'Behold, Your Mother'

"Meet your mother." I love the title of this book, because it echoes some of the most consoling words of Sacred Scripture: "Behold, your mother" (Jn 19:26). Let's look at these words in context.

As he was dying on the Cross, Jesus saw Mary his mother. He also saw John, the beloved disciple, standing near. Then, Jesus said to Mary, "Woman, behold, your son." And to John, "Behold, your mother."

I love that! Why? Because it expresses one of the greatest gifts Jesus could give us, namely, his mother as our spiritual mother. But why is this such a great gift?

Well, let me start off by saying this: The Cross can be a frightening reality. And what can be even more frightening is that Jesus told his disciples, "Take up your cross and follow me" (see Mt 10:38; 16:24; Mk 8:34). In other words, he's telling each of us to lovingly accept suffering.

But who wants to do that? On a natural level, nobody wants to suffer. Yet the reality is, whether we accept it or not, we're all going to experience the weight of suffering. Every one of us. Every day. No wonder Jesus also said, "Take up your cross *daily* and follow me" (Lk 9:23).

Alright, so there's no escaping suffering. And if we're Christians, we're not supposed to rebel against it but rather accept it with love, as Jesus did. Okay, but it's surely not easy. In fact, sometimes suffering can seem too much to bear. Have you ever felt that way? Have you ever felt completely overwhelmed by the crosses in life? Well, what did you do? Chances are, you cried out for Mom (or at least wanted to).

I recently watched a documentary about World War II. During one of the interviews, a veteran explained a situation where a fellow soldier had been shot and left to die because the men in his unit were pinned down by enemy fire. Although they couldn't get to the dying man, they could hear him, and throughout a long night, they had to listen to the slow agony of his death. Repeatedly, he cried out for his mother.

That revelation struck me deeply. Calling out for Mom in times of distress is not just something we did as little kids. Grown men, soldiers on the battlefield — they do it, too. So, yes, it's true: When times are darkest, we need our moms.

Jesus, being fully human, also needed his mom. I believe he needed his mom as he suffered his agony on the Cross. I believe she was for him a precious drop of consolation in the midst of an ocean of bitterness. And I further believe that he wants us to have no less a consolation than he himself had, that he wants us to have his mother as our spiritual mother.

Why? Again, because he knows that he has invited all of us to take up our crosses daily and follow him — and he knows that this is not easy. He knows that life may often seem dark, cold, and full of pain. He knows that sometimes we reach a breaking point in our suffering when we feel we've had enough and are compelled to cry out, "Mom! Momma! Mommy!" And our merciful Savior wants us to know we have a tender, loving, motherly presence in our lives, a woman who will be there to comfort, console, and strengthen us as we continue to follow him.

This book is about coming to better understand the amazing gift from God, the precious gift of our spiritual mother, Mary. While it's just a brief introduction, it's packed with insight and life-changing meaning — which doesn't surprise me. I say this because the author, Dr. Mark Miravalle, was one of my favorite professors at Franciscan University of Steubenville, my alma mater. His contagious love for Mary and clear teaching about her significantly changed my life and the lives of many other students.

I said Dr. Miravalle was my professor — but don't be afraid. This writing is not a college textbook. Rather, it's a brief introduction penned for the "people in the pews." And while there's certainly theological meat to it, it's also full of heart.

I'm so grateful that Dr. Miravalle wrote this book — there's such a need for it. During my travels, I meet so many people who are just awakening to the idea of Mary as their mother. Whether through the Rosary, Marian consecration, or some other way, they seem to be drawing closer to her now as never before. And what a hunger they have! They feel that there's so much they don't know about her, but they want to learn — and learn quickly.

Well, this book is the best brief introduction I've ever read. It's a great way to "meet your mother" by discovering the Church's official teachings on Mary (chapters 1-9) and how she continues to be relevant today (chapters 10-14).

And now, with this new, revised edition, it's even easier to read and grasp Miravalle's Marian wisdom.

So, whether you've already met Mary or hardly know anything about her, I invite you to dig into this treasure of a book. It will help you to receive the gift that Jesus so graciously gave us from the Cross. It will help you to meet and lovingly behold your mother.

Fr. Michael Gaitley, MIC
Director, Association of Marian Helpers
Stockbridge, Massachusetts

Chapter 1

The Whole Truth About Mary

L et's begin with you making a guess: Who do you think penned the following lines about Mary?

> We are all children of Mary ... Mary is the Mother of Jesus and the mother of us all. If Christ is ours, his mother is also ours — she, the Lady above heaven and earth. ... Here passes the woman who is raised far above all women, indeed above the whole human race. ... No woman is like unto thee! Thou art more than an empress or a queen ... blessed above all nobility, wisdom, or saintliness.[1]

Who did you guess? If you're a Catholic, you may have thought it was one of the great Marian saints like St. Bernard of Clairvaux, St. Louis Marie de Montfort, or even the more recent Marian author St. Maximilian Kolbe. If you're not familiar with Catholic authors, you may have guessed some Pope such as St. John Paul II, renowned for his great love of Mary. Well, any of these guesses would have missed the mark.

The answer: Martin Luther, the Father of Protestant Christianity.

So, as you can see, love and appreciation of Mary sometimes appears in unexpected places. In fact, there's a great and sometimes surprising "beauty of diversity" among peoples and cultures who revere Mary.

For instance, it's not widely known that the Mother of Jesus is also the most favored woman in the religion of Islam. Mary is the only woman who has an entire chapter dedicated to her in the Qur'an (the principal religious text of Islam), and is more revered than any woman related to Mohammed, their first prophet, including Mohammed's mother, wives, or daughters (one of whom happens to be named "Fatima"). Although Muslim believers do not hold that Jesus is divine but only a great prophet, they nonetheless accept beliefs similar to Mary's Immaculate Conception, her virginal conception and birth of Jesus, her Assumption, and even her intercession.

Great. But while there are many peoples who revere Mary and believe similar things about her, they don't all fully agree. For instance, Protestants don't believe the same things about Mary as Muslims do. So where can we find the *whole truth* about her?

I believe the whole truth about Mary is found in the four great Marian dogmas taught by the Catholic Church. These teachings about Mary are revealed in the Bible, expressed in Christian Tradition, and solemnly proclaimed by Popes of various Christian ages. Along with the four dogmas, I believe the whole truth about Mary also includes a Marian doctrine that has not yet been raised to the level of dogma. (This doctrine is still an official Catholic teaching, the truth of which has been guaranteed by Catholic authority and has been part of Christian teachings from very beginning.)

The four Marian dogmas all began as seeds given by Jesus in the Bible and in the Tradition of the Apostles that, over time and under the guidance of the Holy Spirit, have developed, ripened, and finally sprung forth as great dogmatic fruits of Christian truth. These four main truths about the Mother of Jesus are as follows: (1) Mary is the Mother of God; (2) Mary is a perpetual virgin; (3) Mary was immaculately conceived; and (4) Mary was bodily assumed into heaven.

The Marian doctrine we'll also cover does not have to do so much with Mary herself but rather with *her special relationship with each one of us*. But before we get to that, let's first examine her relationship to Jesus and the special privileges that flow from that relationship, which are covered in the four Marian dogmas.

Chapter 2

A Creature Gives Birth to Her Creator?

B ack in the fifth century, a doctrinal error or "heresy" arose concerning "who" and "what" is Jesus Christ. A man named Nestorius was spreading the mistaken notion that Jesus Christ was essentially two separate persons — one divine and the other, human. This heresy ("Nestorianism") might sound like no big deal at first, but this mistake about Jesus would be nothing less than the difference between our salvation and the lack thereof!

What, then, does Nestorianism have to do with Mary? Well, Nestorius refused to call Mary the "Mother of God" (or "*Theotokos*" in Greek) but only "Mother of Christ" (or "*Christotokos*") because he believed Mary to be mother of only the human person, Christ, and not of the divine person, Jesus, who is both God and man. It was actually Nestorius's refusal to call Mary the "*Theotokos*" (which literally means "God-bearer) that gave the Church the heads-up that Nestorius was really teaching something wrong about Jesus. (Mary leads people to the truth about Jesus, and she protects them from falling into error.)

The Christian truth is that Jesus Christ is not two separate persons, but only one divine person with two natures: one that is entirely divine, and the other that is entirely human. You can never separate these divine and human natures into two different persons without doing great damage to our salvation. For example, if Jesus is two separate persons, then who died on Calvary to save us? If you answer, "Only the human person," then we have just lost our redemption! No human death could satisfy the price for all of humanity's sins. If you say, "The divine person," then you are saying the infinite God can be killed in his infinite spirit and divine personhood — another whoops! Only the free and loving death of a God-man, whose suffering and death would provide an infinite offering to the Heavenly Father, could compensate for the infinite offenses of humanity.

By the way, you don't want to start a heresy for several reasons. It leads people into error; it can cause a great crisis of faith; and if that weren't enough, they might name it after you!

Let's look at a contemporary example of the same process that happened back in the fifth century. Let's say after a typical Sunday Mass, you approach a typical Catholic coming out of church. He goes to Sunday Mass, and while he's not steeped in the Catholic Catechism (the summary of Catholic beliefs), fundamentally, he's a committed member of the Church. You, then, go up to the person and say, "Excuse me, can I ask you a question? I know Mass is over and you're ready to go, but just a quick question?"

"Sure."

"Who is Jesus Christ?" you ask.

"Well, Jesus is God."

"Anything else?"

"Well, yeah. He's God and man."

You respond, "Yes, Jesus is God and man. Okay, that's good. Now answer this question for me: How many persons, how many natures, how many intellects, how many wills, how many souls did Jesus have?"

At this point, the person says, "Look, buddy, it's donut Sunday. I gotta get movin' here."

You retort, "Ok, one last question before you hit the donuts. What if I were to say to you that you can't call Mary the 'Mother of God'?"

To this, the average Catholic parishioner replies, "Oh, no, that's wrong. Mary is the mother of Jesus; Jesus is God; therefore, you have to call Mary the Mother of God." Then, with a certain sense of accomplishment, off he goes to the donut line in the parish hall — and his answer would have been right!

That, in essence, is what happened in the early Church. When people heard of Nestorius's mistaken teaching about Jesus applied to Mary, they clearly saw the error about Jesus.

In truth as in life, Mary protects and serves her Son.

In response to Nestorius, St. Cyril of Alexandria led the Council of Ephesus in 431 (an "ecumenical" council, whose decisions are binding on the entire Church when approved by the Pope), which condemned the errors of Nestorius and solemnly declared Mary as the "Mother of God." At that council, *Mary's divine motherhood becomes the first Marian dogma, the first solemnly defined truth about Mary, in the history of the Church.*

But how can a creature become mother of her own Creator? Let's define our terms.

A mother is classically defined as a woman who gives to her offspring a nature identical to her own. (I wouldn't suggest using this definition on a Mother's Day card, but it's still accurate.)

What precisely did Mary give to Jesus? His divine nature? No. His divine personhood? No. Those both came from the Heavenly Father as the divine Word was begotten from the Father from all eternity.

What, then, did Mary give to Jesus? *She gave him a nature identical to her own* — in this exceptional, one-time-in-history case, she gave him an immaculate ("flawless") human nature (as we'll discuss shortly).

Yes, and that human nature of Jesus was inseparably (*hypostatically*, to use the classic term in theology) united to the divine person and the divine nature of Jesus from the moment the Holy Spirit infused the eternal Word (God, the Second Person of the Trinity) into the womb of Mary.

So we conclude: Mary gave birth to a Son who was truly God. She gave Jesus a human nature identical to her own. (Remember the definition of motherhood.) This is why we rightly call Mary the "Mother of God."

The title Mother of God does not, of course, mean that Mary is "mother of the Father" or "mother of the Holy Spirit." These ideas would also be heresies. As a creature, she cannot exist before her Creator. But she can be the God-designed means for the Second Person of the Trinity to become man at a given time in human history in the event we call the "Incarnation." Mary is Mother of God the Son made man, that is, Mother of Jesus Christ, who is truly God.

The Bible clearly reveals that Mary is the Mother of Jesus, who is the Son of God:

> In the sixth month, the angel Gabriel was sent by God to a city of Galilee named Nazareth, to a virgin...and the virgin's name was Mary ... and he

came to her and said: "Hail, full of grace, the Lord is with you! ... you will conceive and bear a son, and you shall call his name, Jesus. He will be great and will be called the Son of the Most High" ... And Mary said, "Behold I am the handmaid of the Lord. Let it be done to me according to your word" (Lk 1:26-38).

Saint Paul's letter to the Galatians further reveals that God became man through a woman: "When in the fullness of time, God sent his Son, born of a woman" (Gal 4:4).

This first Marian dogma of Mary as Mother of God is likewise enthusiastically defended by the Father of Christian Protestantism, Martin Luther:

She is rightly called not only the mother of the man, the human nature of Jesus, but also the Mother of God. It is certain that Mary is the Mother of the real and true God. Men have crowded all her glory into a single phrase: the Mother of God. No one can say anything greater about her though he had as many tongues as there are leaves on trees.[2]

Motherhood is such a beautiful thing. And when God himself calls you, "Mother," well, that's something heavenly.

Chapter 3

The 'Perpetual' Virgin

The concept of virginity today is rather mysterious and oftentimes confused. It is frequently perceived as a big "no" to the beauty of human sexuality. In reality, at least in a Christian context, virginity is actually a big and sacrificial "yes" to God's gift of the body and sexuality, as well as to the greatest possible imitation of the life of Jesus.

The second dogma concerning Mary is her *threefold virginity*. The historical setting for this Marian proclamation was the First Lateran Council in 649, where Pope Martin I proclaimed Mary as being virginal in three key ways: (1) *before* the birth of Jesus, (2) *during* the birth of Jesus, and (3) *after* the birth of Jesus.

Before looking specifically at Mary's exceptional life of virginity, let's turn our attention to the vocation of lifelong Christian virginity.

For the Christian, to live such a life or to make a vow of perpetual virginity is in no way to imply that human sexuality is a "bad thing." Quite the contrary, Christians who willfully and committedly live their lives without sexual relations greatly value the gift of their bodies and their sexuality — so much so that they decide to give the gift of their bodies and the possibility of sexuality back to

God as a personal gift to him. The priest or religious sister or consecrated virgin is not negating the gift of the body and sexuality. Rather, they are acknowledging their beauty and value, saying out of gratitude and fidelity to God, "I give the gift of sexuality back to You, God, in my best effort to imitate the life of Jesus."

As Jesus lived a life of virginity in service to the mission given him by the Heavenly Father, priests and nuns also seek to do so. Lifetime virginity is not a "no" to the value of sexuality but rather a "yes." Therefore, we should see it as an extremely valuable and precious gift that celibates, out of love and sacrifice, give back to the Creator (like a small child's gift to their father on Father's Day, which is actually paid for by the father himself!).

Now, with this general understanding of Christian virginity, let's explore the three aspects of Mary's perfect, lifelong virginity.

Virginity Before the Birth of Jesus

The first aspect of Mary's Virginity, that she was virginal before the birth of Christ, is the fulfillment of the beautiful prophecy given by the Old Testament prophet Isaiah more than 600 years before the coming of Jesus: "Behold, a virgin will conceive and bear a son and his name shall be called Emmanuel" (Is 7:14). Mary conceived Jesus without the assistance of man, for God the Son was conceived in the womb of Mary by the power of the Holy Spirit.

It is a pillar of Christian belief that Mary became pregnant with Jesus through the power of the Holy Spirit (the Third Person of the Blessed Trinity) without the cooperation of a man. The Apostles' Creed (a formula of

Christian belief that dates back to the first two centuries) teaches that Jesus was "conceived by the Holy Spirit, born of the Virgin Mary."

The Bible reveals Mary's virginity in the words of St. Luke (one of the four Gospel writers), "The virgin's name was Mary" (Lk 1:27) and in Mary's own words after the angel Gabriel states, in a message from God, that she will conceive and bear the "Son of the Most High": *"How shall this be, for I know not man"* (Lk 1:34). We will return to these words of Mary and their full meaning shortly.

Virginity During the Birth of Jesus

The second aspect of Mary's complete virginity is her virginity *during* the birth of Christ. This aspect is commonly referred to by early Christian writers as the "miraculous birth" of Jesus Christ. The Fathers of the Church, those remarkable early preachers and teachers of Christianity, used this beautiful image: As light passes through glass without harming the glass, so, too, at the appointed time, *Jesus left the womb of Mary in a miraculous manner without violation to Mary's physical virginity.*

Why? Why would God perform a miracle so as to allow Mary to give birth to Jesus without harming her physical virginity? Well, first of all, Mary's physical virginity is an outward sign of her perfect interior virginity — her perfect "yes" to Jesus in heart and in body. In what is called the "Theology of the Body," a series of insights on the God-given meaning and value of the body as understood by St. Pope John Paul II, he teaches that "the body expresses the person." Applied in this case, it means that Mary's intact physical virginity is a concrete sign and symbol of her perfect interior gift of her entire self — including her body — to Jesus. Mary's physical virginity is a physical expression of perfect Christian discipleship to and imitation of Jesus.

The bottom line: During the one time in human history when God becomes man and wants to have, simultaneously, one woman be a 'perfect mother' and a 'perfect virgin,' you have to expect exceptions! You have to expect and accept miracles.

We must also keep in mind that because Mary was immaculately conceived and free from Original Sin and all of its effects (we're getting to that dogma next), Mary could not suffer labor pains in giving birth, since labor pains are an effect of the fall of Adam and Eve (see Gen 3:16).

Mary would not have her perfect physical virginity disturbed by the birth of her Son since Jesus, above all others, appreciated and desired to protect his Mother's marvelous virginity of heart and body. This is confirmed in the famous "tome" or letter of St. Pope Leo the Great back in 449 where he teaches, "She brought him forth without loss to her virginity, just as she conceived him without loss to her virginity."[3]

The teachings of Vatican II and the *Catechism of the Catholic Church* articulate this same truth by saying that the birth of Jesus "did not diminish his mother's virginal integrity, but sanctified it."[4]

Listen to this testimony of Mary's miraculous birth of Jesus, as well as of her lifelong virginity, from another major Protestant founder, the Swiss author, Huldrych Zwingli: "I firmly believe according to the words of the Gospel, that this pure virgin brought forth for us the Son of God and remained a virgin, pure and intact, in childbirth and also after the birth, for all eternity."[5]

Virginity After the Birth of Jesus

The third aspect of Mary's virginity is her virginity *after* the birth of Christ. This aspect teaches that Mary had neither marital relations with Joseph nor any other children besides Jesus.

Once again, the great early Christian commentators known as the "Church Fathers" saw in Mary's response to the angel Gabriel ("How will this be, since I know not man") an implicit reference to a *vow of virginity* that Mary had made prior to the event of this Annunciation. Those words "I know not man" (a Hebrew expression for not having intercourse) refer to a permanent commitment of Mary's heart, not just something that had not yet happened.

Take this example. If a person offers you a cigarette, but you've made a permanent commitment not to smoke, you would reply kindly, "Oh, no thank you. I don't smoke." Now in your response, you're not only saying "I don't want to smoke now," but you're also communicating that "I don't smoke" as a permanent habit or disposition. So, too, with Mary (not with smoking — but with virginity).

Her words "I know not man" don't only mean "I don't want to know man now" or "I haven't known man yet" but more accurately "I do not know man" as a permanent commitment, a lifetime vow of virginity. Surely, Mary doesn't mean by the question or statement "How shall this be, for I know not man" that she doesn't know where babies come from! No, the Church Fathers are right. Mary does not "know man" due to her vowed life of perpetual virginity.

While we're here, let's also quickly respond to a common objection to Mary's lifelong virginity. It has to do with references in the Bible to the "brothers"[6] of Jesus, which leads some to conclude that these are references to literal blood brothers of Jesus, which calls into question Mary's perpetual virginity.

The biblical word for brother in Greek (the predominant language of the New Testament) is *"adelphos,"* which is translated not only as "brother" but also "cousin," "near relative," or even "kinsman," someone from your hometown. The biblical term "brother" is in no sense limited to blood relations. The same goes for the Hebrew word for "brother" in the Old Testament *"ah"* — it means, brother, cousin, close friend, near relative, or someone from your hometown or tribe. In fact, in other passages in the Bible where the term "brother" is used, through the context of the passage, it absolutely does not and cannot refer to blood brother.[7]

The Bible is referring here either to cousins of Jesus on Joseph's side, or, more generally, to followers or disciples of Jesus. The word "brother" only makes sense in understanding how that word was used in the time of Jesus and actually, how it is still used today.

Obviously, we commonly use the words "brothers" and "sisters" in a variety of ways that are not in any way referring to literal blood brothers and sisters: for example, fraternity brothers, sorority sisters, or more generally, "brothers and sisters in the Lord." Jesus directly and obviously uses the "brothers" reference to talk about spiritual discipleship: "My mother and my brothers are those who hear the word of God and keep it" (Lk 8:21). That's either one massive biological family of over 2 billion people today, or it's referring to the spiritual brotherhood of all Christians.

Believe me, if Jesus had blood brothers (which he didn't), then Jesus at Calvary could never have given Mary to the care of John at Calvary (see Jn 19:26-27), a friend, rather than to her true biological sons (a huge violation of Jewish custom).

No, Mary's virginity was lifelong. Jesus was the first-born (and only-born) of the Father and the first-born (and only-born) of Mary.

Let me, once again, quote Protestant founder, Martin Luther (who, by the way, wrote his doctoral dissertation on Mary's *Magnificat* [Hymn of Praise] and asked for her intercession to help him complete it well!) in his clear defense of Mary's perpetual virginity: "Christ our Savior was the real and natural fruit of Mary's virginal womb. This was without the cooperation of a man, and she remained a virgin after that."[8]

Luther's colleague and Protestant co-founder, John Calvin, stated that the early Christian writer Helvidius "showed himself ignorant in saying that Mary had several sons because mention is made in some passages of the brothers of Christ" and then proceeded to translate the "brothers" reference from the Bible as cousins, or near relatives, but absolutely not as "blood brothers."[9]

Virginity is a "yes" to God, to the value of sexuality, and to being the best possible disciple of Jesus. Mary gave Jesus this virginal "yes" in mind, spirit, *and body*, her whole life long.

Chapter 4

The 'Immaculate' Conception

The Church's dogmas about Mary reach out and touch many areas of contemporary life and culture — even professional American football!

In 1972, Franco Harris, a running back for the Pittsburgh Steelers, made an amazing, near-miraculous catch and subsequent run to win a playoff game against the Oakland Raiders. Many commentators have called it the greatest single play in the history of professional football. What was this extraordinary catch nicknamed for all pro football perpetuity? The "Immaculate Reception."

Well, this is a sports pun named after the greatest single moment of grace for a human being in the history of humanity: the "Immaculate Conception."

The third dogma that the Catholic Church has proclaimed about Mary is precisely her Immaculate Conception. This dogma teaches that *Mary was conceived without Original Sin or any of its effects* by the "merits" of Jesus Christ, as we'll discuss. Positively put, this truth reveals that Mary was "full of grace," in the words of the Archangel Gabriel, from the moment of her conception.

On December 8, 1854, Blessed Pope Pius IX used the "charism" or gift of papal infallibility (a protection of the Holy Spirit from error regarding faith and morals that Catholics believe Jesus gave to Peter and his successors, the Popes) to solemnly define the dogma of the Immaculate Conception:

> We declare, pronounce, and define that the doctrine which holds that the most blessed Virgin Mary, at the first instant of her conception, was preserved immune from all stain of sin, by a singular grace and privilege of the Omnipotent God, in view of the merits of Jesus Christ, Savior of the human race, was revealed by God and must be firmly and constantly believed by all the faithful.[10]

This profound Marian truth has been passed down through what we call "Apostolic Tradition" (the teachings of Jesus to the Apostles, which were then transmitted to their successors, the Pope and bishops, under the Holy Spirit's guidance). As we'll see, the essence of the dogma of the Immaculate Conception was taught within the first centuries of Christianity.

Church Fathers from the early centuries[11] compared Mary to Eve's state of created purity and innocence. In other words, Mary was as Eve was before her participation in the Original Sin with Adam and her resulting fall from grace. Obviously, before Eve sinned with Adam in what we now call the "Original Sin," she was entirely free from Original Sin and all its negative effects! Another Church Father, St. Ambrose,[12] taught in the late 300s that Mary was "altogether without the stain of sin." By the sixth century, she was called "Immaculate"[13]; and by the ninth century, Mary was understood to have been "conceived by a sanctifying action."[14] This is really remarkable, since the common biological teachings of the day did not even universally accept that human life begins at conception until several centuries later!

So you can see that while the papal definition of Blessed Pope Pius IX was a true development of this truth in the form of an official dogma, it was by no means the beginning of the truth. The Immaculate Conception of Mary, although understood better over time within the Church, is a doctrine that was certainly known within Christian faith and life throughout the first thousand years of Christianity.

In the Bible, the Immaculate Conception of Mary can be seen implicitly in the famous passage of Genesis 3:15 (known as the "*Protoevangelium*" or "First Gospel"), the first reference to Jesus as the future Redeemer of the world. After Adam and Eve commit their sin of disobedience, God addresses the serpent (who represents Satan) and says: "I will put enmity between you and the woman, and between your seed and her seed. She shall crush your head and you shall lie in wait for her heel."[15] Notice that God himself places "enmity," which is a total and absolute opposition, between the woman and the serpent and their respective offspring, or "seeds." (By the way, have you ever thought about how strange it is to talk about the "seed" of a woman rather than the seed of a man — already a hint of Mary's virginal conception of Jesus!)

Now, how do we know the "woman" referred to in the passage is ultimately Mary? Because Eve did not give birth to the "seed of victory." Since the seed who is victorious over Satan and sin must be Jesus, *the "woman" in this*

prophecy who gives birth to the future savior must be Mary.
Let's look more closely at what's going on here.

First, God puts a total, radical opposition between the woman and the serpent. Then, what does he say? "She will crush your head" (Gen 3:15). Because of Mary's Immaculate Conception being completely in opposition to Satan (in fact, in the passage, Mary has exactly the same opposition to Satan as Jesus does to sin — it's a parallel opposition), Mary's future role with and under Jesus in the redemptive defeat of Satan and his seed is subtly revealed in this text.

Regardless of the issue of the pronoun, (whether it be "she" will crush your head, traditional translation, or "he" will crush your head, more recent translation), what's clear is that the woman is intimately involved with Jesus, the victorious seed, in the saving victory over Satan and sin.

In the New Testament, we find more evidence to support the dogma of the Immaculate Conception. For instance, in Luke 1:28, the angel Gabriel comes to Mary and greets her with a new name, "Hail, *full of grace!*" The Greek translation here is really fascinating and helpful to fully appreciate this passage. (I won't be throwing any more Greek your way — just this once.)

The Greek verb for "full of grace" is *kecharitomene*, a perfect passive participle (stay with me here) that grammatically refers to an action completed entirely *in the past* but with a relevance to the present. This means the Angel Gabriel refers to Mary with a name or phrase that points to an action of grace that was perfectly completed in the past yet is still important for the present. What completely perfecting action of grace in the past did Mary experience? You got it — the Immaculate Conception! Beautiful! That's worth a little Greek grammar.

But how is Mary preserved from Original Sin by the "merits" of Jesus? Mary's Immaculate Conception is a higher form of salvation accomplished by Jesus than the rest of us receive (if we so choose). We are born in a deprived state due to the Original Sin of our first parents. We have to be baptized for the life of sanctifying grace to return to our souls, for us to receive the saving graces of Jesus. Mary, on the other hand, was "saved" by receiving a fullness of grace at the moment of her conception, graces that also come from the redeeming death of Jesus on the Cross. (God, who is outside of time, can apply the graces of redemption to Mary at the moment of her conception.)

In short, *Mary, as a daughter of Adam and Eve, needed to be saved, and she was saved by the grace of Jesus Christ — applied to her soul at the moment of conception.*[16]

Again, I want to quote Martin Luther in support of Mary's Immaculate Conception (taken here from his personal prayer book of 1522). He says: "She is full of grace. Proclaimed to be entirely without sin, God's grace fills her with everything good and makes her devoid of all evil."[17]

Saint Maximilian Kolbe, a Polish priest-saint known for giving up his life to save a married man in an Auschwitz concentration camp during World War II, adds some stunning insights about Mary's Immaculate Conception that I want to share here. They have to do with what Our Lady said about herself in Lourdes, France.

In Lourdes, the Mother of Jesus appeared to the young seer Bernadette Soubirous. Mary answered Bernadette's repeated question "Who are you?" with the powerful response, "I am the Immaculate Conception." Saint Maximilian understood that Mary was saying something more than just "believe in the Immaculate Conception," or even "I was immaculately conceived." Mary was saying something about her very person, her very being.

Saint Maximilian struggled to make sense of this, since it almost seemed to give Mary the appearance of divinity. After years of such struggle, he realized the solution: There are two "Immaculate Conceptions," both intimately connected. Father Michael Gaitley, MIC, describes Kolbe's discovery:

> Mary is the *created* Immaculate Conception and the Holy Spirit is the *uncreated* Immaculate Conception. In other words, before there was the *created* Immaculate Conception (Mary), for all eternity, there is the *uncreated* Immaculate Conception, the One who for all eternity "springs" from God the Father and God the Son as an uncreated conception of Love ... .
>
> Now, the Holy Spirit is a "conception" in the sense of being the Life and Love that springs from the love of the Father and the Son — in some analogous way, there's the conception of children who "spring" from the love of husband and wife. The Holy Spirit is an "immaculate" conception because, being God, he is obviously without sin. And finally, the Holy Spirit is an "eternal, uncreated" conception because, again, he is God.[18]

This truth about the Holy Spirit explains Mary's words at Lourdes. Mary *is* the (created) Immaculate Conception because of her union with the uncreated Immaculate Conception. Saint Maximilian described their union as follows:

It is above all an interior union, a union of her essence with the "essence" of the Holy Spirit. The Holy Spirit dwells in her, lives in her. This was true from the first instant of her existence. It was always true; it will always be true.

In what does this life of the Spirit in Mary consist? He himself is uncreated Love in her; the Love of the Father and of the Son, the Love by which God loves himself, the very Love of the Most Holy Trinity ... the Holy Spirit lives in the soul of the Immaculate, in the depths of her very being. He makes her fruitful, from the very first instant of her existence, all during her life, and for all eternity.

This eternal "Immaculate Conception" (which is the Holy Spirit) produces in an immaculate manner divine life itself in the womb (or depths) of Mary's soul, making her the Immaculate Conception, the human Immaculate Conception.[19]

Saint Maximilian further explains how appropriate it is for Mary to take on the name of her Divine Spouse:

... If among human beings the wife takes the name of her husband because she belongs to him, is one with him, becomes equal to him and is, with him, the source of new life, with how much greater reason should the name of the Holy Spirit, who is the divine Immaculate Conception, be used as the name of her in whom he lives as uncreated Love, the principle of life in the whole supernatural order of grace? [20]

Mary, of course, is not divine, but by calling herself the Immaculate Conception, she was telling the world that she, in some real way, is *full of grace*, by her very God-given nature. Just as God, on the divine level, said to Moses, "I am who I am," which describes his divine nature as God who has always existed; so also on the human level, in saying "I am the Immaculate Conception," Mary describes her nature as *created full of the grace of God* without any effects of Original Sin. She's a "new creation," as the Church Fathers would say.

Awesome and beautiful! God's finest masterpiece, beyond the greatest natural wonders of the world and even beyond the galaxies of stars in the cosmos, is the creature who received the highest level of sanctifying grace (which is a participation in the very life and love of God) at the moment of her conception. Second only to her Son's own sacred humanity, nothing on earth is or ever will be more holy.

Chapter 5

Did Mary Die?

L et's start with another question: Do you think Mary
died? Some of you may be quick to respond, "Yes,
of course — she was human!" Others may retort, "No,
she didn't — because death is a result of sin, and Mary
was conceived without Original Sin or its effects." We'll see
that there is yet a third possibility, one that not only incor-
porates the truth about the Immaculate Conception but
also Mary's perfect imitation of the life of Jesus. (If you're
stuck on this, that's the idea — read on!)

The fourth Marian dogma proclaimed by the Church
is Mary's Assumption. It was proclaimed by Venerable
Pope Pius XII on November 1, 1950, and states: "The
Immaculate Mother of God, the ever-Virgin Mary, having
completed the course of her earthly life, was assumed body
and soul into heavenly glory."[21]

In many ways, the Assumption of Mary body and soul
into heaven at the end of her life on earth just makes sense
— if you understand her Immaculate Conception and its
positive consequences.

Back to Genesis 3:15. Remember that because Mary
was free from Original Sin, she would not experience any
of the negative effects of Original Sin. Well, one big effect

of Original Sin is death by the "corruption" or physical breakdown of the body. Yes, death and disease enter the world because of sin.[22] So, the woman who was preserved from the effects of that first human sin would, consequently, neither experience bodily decay nor the ultimate physical failure we call "death" — at least not death because of the failure of the human body.

The immaculate mother of Jesus would end her life on earth not because of cancer, heart attack, or simply old age — but only when her Son wanted her home with him in heaven.

From the Bible, we can see how Mary's bodily Assumption into heaven comes as a common sense result of being without Original Sin (see Gen 3:15 again). The same holds true when we consider the greeting of the Angel, "Hail, full of grace" (Lk 1:28), because a creature with a fullness of grace and no sin would not experience the effects of sin in the body — for example, a physical decay, leading to death. We also have the lovely reference to both Jesus' Ascension (something he does by his own divine power) and Mary's Assumption (something she passively receives from God) in Psalm 132:8, where the Psalmist says, "Arise, O Lord, into your resting place, you and the Ark which you have sanctified." As Mary is the "New Ark" who carried Jesus inside of her, this passage also foreshadows her bodily Assumption into heaven.

Still more biblical support for Mary's Assumption comes from Revelation 11:19, with the vision of the Ark of the Covenant now in heaven (Mary being the fulfillment of the Old Testament Ark that contained the stone tablets of the Ten Commandments, a jar of manna, and Aaron's rod because Jesus is even *holier* than these signs of God's presence). The vision of the Ark of the Covenant in heaven is immediately followed by a vision of a "woman clothed with the sun" (Rev 12:1) who gives birth to the "male child," the ruler of all nations. This means that this "woman" must be Mary. Who else gave birth to the "male child," ruler of all nations? Also, she is already seen in heaven, both as the New Ark and as the Woman united with her Son and crowned with 12 stars as Queen in the Kingdom of her Son, the King. (More on her Queenship to come.)

Mary's Assumption is a sign of hope for us all. It's tells us that one day, God willing, at the end of time and after the final judgment,[23] we will be judged worthy to have our bodies united with our souls in heaven for all eternity.

Now back to the million-dollar question: Did Mary die?

Let's imagine that we are all participating at an ecumenical council of the Church, and you are a voting member of this Council. (Of course, this can't happen, and we would all have to be dispensed for not being bishops, which is impossible, but let's just go with this for a moment.) The simple question up for vote is this: "Did Mary die?" What would your vote be — Yes or No?

Well, let's establish the parameters to the question.

In 1949, you had two groups of theologians responding to this question, known as (1) the "Mortalists" and (2) the "Immortalists." (That's "Immortalists," not "Immoralists.")

The Mortalists took the position that Mary did experience a three-day separation of soul and body in departing from this earthly life as an expression of her perfect imitation of and discipleship to her Son, Jesus, who also experienced a three-day separation of soul and body from Good Friday to Easter Sunday. After this three-day separation of soul and body, her body was assumed by angels into heaven, and her body and soul were then united in heaven for all eternity.

The Immortalists took the counter position that Mary never experienced any temporary separation of soul and body before being brought into heaven by God, but she was simply brought to heaven, body and soul united, at the end of her life.

Now remember the key parameter: No Catholic can hold that Mary died through a *corruption of the body*. Why? Because of her Immaculate Conception.

Both groups waited with great anticipation for the Pope, Pius XII, to settle this issue once and for all in the papal definition of the Assumption as dogma. Well, on November 1, 1950, Pius XII in his full authority as successor of Peter and Head of the Church on earth, solemnly declared on this issue of Mary's death — (drum roll) — absolutely — (more drum roll ...) — *nothing*.

What? Why not? Because the Pope correctly decided that Mary's death was not an essential part of the dogma of Mary's bodily Assumption into heaven. (This shows that Popes use their papal infallibility carefully and sparingly — only for the essential doctrinal pronouncements.)

Since that time, St. Pope John Paul II did discuss the "death of Mary" in a teaching,[24] where he said it was in line with the Church's Eastern tradition of the "Dormition" of Mary (as St. Paul uses the expression, "those asleep in Christ," referring to death).[25] The strong overall Christian Tradition is that Mary did die, but (remember the parameters) not because of bodily decay but in a perfect following of the life of her Son (something only the Heavenly Father could arrange).

These, then, are the four dogmas that have already been solemnly declared about Jesus' Mother: her divine Motherhood, her Perpetual Virginity, her Immaculate Conception, and her bodily Assumption.

Now, and only now, are we ready to discuss the final official teaching about Mary.

Yes, we had to start on the firm foundation of Mary's relationship with Jesus, which historically and theologically came first. After all, Jesus is obviously more important than us. And this is more than okay, because we will receive our relationship with Mary (if we so choose) on the basis of Jesus' relationship with her.

There remains, then, one doctrine, one official Church teaching regarding Mary that has yet to be defined as a dogma. This teaching ought to be fascinating to our minds and — I hope — near and dear to our hearts. This Marian teaching is the one directed specifically to you (and to me, too). It is the doctrine concerning Mary's relationship to the human family, *her relationship to each one of us.*

Chapter 6

Our Spiritual Mother

When I was a child (centuries ago), one of my favorite books was called *Are You My Mother?* It is a sweet little book about a baby bird who had hatched while his mother was away. He began walking around and asking anything and everything he encountered, from construction cranes to other animals, "Are you my mother?" The story ends happily when he finally finds his true mother and is overwhelmed with joy by her loving presence.

Now, even though our quest here is not a fictional child's book but a serious adult search for the truth about Mary, the Mother of Jesus, and whether she is, in a spiritual but real sense, *our true mother,* there are certain parallels. To be open to the possibility of finding a true mother, we have to have not a child-ish but a child-like openness.

We are beings that are not our own creators. We are beings that have God as our Father, and perhaps this Heavenly Father wanted us to experience a type of spiritual mother as well. This, my friends, appears to be the case, if we offer an open heart to the words of the Heavenly Father's first Child: Jesus, his divine Son and our divine Brother.

Now, I'm going to refer to the New Testament here as a source of revealed truth from God without making the overall case for the truth of Christianity itself. While I'd love to make that case, I would want to do it thoroughly and reasonably, and here is just not the appropriate place to do it. (That's a book unto itself.)

The same must be said to Christians reading this concise work who are not Catholic. Although the interpretation of the words of Jesus that I will give here is the interpretation shared by the early Christian commentators (those great Church Fathers again) as well as the Popes of Christian history, I will not give a detailed "apologetic" explanation and defense of this passage as I have done in other books.[26] Instead, I am just going to *invite you* to have an open mind and heart to these words of Jesus, and see if, deep down in that wonderful soul God gave you, you feel a sense of peace with what Jesus says about his mother and about you.

When Jesus was dying on Calvary to offer his life as a ransom, a payment, for our sins to the Heavenly Father, right before the greatest single act of sacrificial love in all of human history was about to be accomplished, Jesus gave us *one last gift*. How important is this gift? It is so important that he gives it to us right at the very end.

Looking down from the Cross, Jesus sees his mother, who has not left his side during this historic sacrifice, and his "beloved disciple" John, the youngest apostle and the only one who has shown his loyalty by staying with Jesus during his crucifixion. Then, right before he declares, "It is finished," Jesus gives each of us and all of us the greatest gift, after our salvation, that he could give: *He gives us his own mother to be our spiritual mother.*

"Woman, behold, your son," Jesus says to Mary (Jn 19:26). That Jesus refers to his own mother as "Woman" tells us that she holds a type of office that goes beyond just their own personal mother-son relationship. She, Mary, is the "Woman" of Genesis (3:15), the "Woman" of Cana (Jn 2:4), the "Woman" of Revelation (12:1) — the "Woman" of the Bible. And now, her motherly role with Jesus in the work of salvation is expanded — to us.

But how do we know that these words from Jesus to Mary don't simply refer to John as an individual? Because everything Jesus does from the Cross has a universal impact! Jesus didn't just die for John, but for you and me and for every single human being who has ever walked the face of the earth or will in the future. No, Jesus' universal act of Redemption on Calvary affects every human being — *and so does his gift of Mary's spiritual motherhood.*

Jesus then turned to the young John and said, "Behold, your mother" (Jn 19:27). Yes, Mary becomes the beloved disciple's spiritual mother and the spiritual mother of all who seek to be "beloved disciples" of Jesus. Jesus dies for all humanity at this historical moment, and he offers humanity the two great fruits of redemptive suffering (from his "Passion") before he dies: *Jesus offers us the gift of eternal life through faith in him, and he gives Mary to each of us as a personal gift* — whether or not we choose to accept these gifts is up to us.

These two gifts of divine love, so beautifully intermingled at Calvary, should be received by all, especially when they come from Jesus and at such a great price.

Let's look at the beloved disciple's response to this extraordinary gift from the dying Jesus. The Bible tells us that John took Mary "into his own home" (Jn 19:27).

Maybe that's what we need to do — take Mary into our homes, into our hearts, into our spiritual and interior lives, into our families, *into our present world situation.*

But how specifically is the Mother of Jesus a "spiritual mother" to each of us personally? Well, as we'll see, in the same ways that a good mother is specifically a mother to us in the natural order of things, so, too, is Mary a mother to us in the spiritual order of things. Mary is, as the Second Vatican Council put it, "a mother to us in the order of grace."[27]

"Mary, are you my mother?" Let's continue the search and see.

Chapter 7

Is Mary a 'Co-redeemer'?

I must say I am excited about this chapter! (Not that I wasn't excited about the other chapters, because I personally find the truth about the Mother of Jesus pretty exciting in general.) But I am particularly excited about this chapter, because it deals with one of the most potentially confusing parts of the truth about Mary that is also the easiest to clarify. And this clarifying process really starts with identifying a "call" or duty that is shared by all Christians.

Co-redeemers in Christ

Let's start with one of the most mysterious passages of the New Testament. This is where Christians are called to imitate St. Paul's example to "make up what is lacking in the sufferings of Christ for the sake of his body, which is the Church" (Col 1:24).

That's right! That's what the Bible actually says: Christians are all called to "*make up what is lacking in the sufferings of Christ.*"

At first glance, this passage of St. Paul looks pretty presumptuous — and in two ways. First, it seems to infer that there was something "lacking" or inadequate in the sufferings of Jesus. Secondly, it implies that we, weak and fallen creatures that we are, are called to "make up" for "what is lacking" in the sufferings of Jesus (almost like it's a good thing we're around to make up for what Jesus didn't finish, right?). That sounds blasphemous. But what does St. Paul really mean?

Here we have to make a distinction between two aspects of human salvation: first, the historic *obtaining* of saving graces infinitely and superabundantly accomplished by Jesus through his life, death, and Resurrection; second, the *release and acceptance* of those saving graces to human hearts of all ages. The first (what some theologians call "objective redemption") is the infinite acquiring of the graces by which everyone can be *redeemed* or "bought back" from sin and Satan by Jesus' loving suffering and death. This saving act of Jesus has absolutely nothing "lacking" to it. On the contrary, the graces Jesus obtained for us on the Cross are not only enough to pay for the sins of the entire world in justice to the Heavenly Father, but they are infinitely beyond the amount of graces necessary.

It's the second aspect of human salvation that St. Paul is referring to: the release and acceptance of the saving graces of Jesus by human beings. It is precisely this part of salvation in which the Bible calls each Christian to take an active role.

If you and I are each a member of Christ's mystical body (in virtue of our Baptism and Christian faith), then we get to play an extremely important role in the release of the infinite graces of Jesus to the people around us today.

How do we do this? By offering our prayers, sacrifices, and sufferings with the intention of uniting them to the sufferings of Jesus. These spiritual offerings become supernaturally fruitful in releasing a portion of those saving graces of Jesus to the hearts of our brothers and sisters in the world.

This is why St. Paul called us "co-workers with God" (1 Cor 3:9). Saint Pope John Paul II called all Christians to fulfill their roles as "co-redeemers in Christ"[28] and to express this joyful and co-redemptive role of Christians in joining Jesus, the one and only divine Redeemer, in this work of saving souls. In a similar way, Pope Benedict XVI called all Christians to become "redeemers in the Redeemer."[29]

At this point, you may be saying, "Wait a minute — I thought this chapter was going to be about Mary being a 'co-redeemer'? Where is Mary's role in all this?" Great question.

Mary as a 'Co-redemptrix'

If all Christians are called to cooperate with Jesus in the great mission of human salvation, if we can rightly be called "co-redeemers in Christ" for joining Jesus in offering our prayers and sufferings in union with his sufferings to save souls, then, clearly, *Mary can also be called a "co-redeemer" with Jesus.*

Did she not cooperate with Jesus in the work of human salvation? Did she not unite her sufferings with those of Jesus for souls?

Yes, she did. And what's more, *Mary is a co-redeemer with Jesus in ways unlike any other co-redeemer.*

Before we continue with this point, let's take a quick look at the term that has been used in Christian Tradition for Mary for over 700 years to identify her unique role with Jesus in the work of human redemption. It is the title "Co-redemptrix."

Now before your knee jerks in response to this Co-redemptrix title, let's remember a few things. First, all Christians, once again, can and should be fulfilling the role of being "co-redeemers" with Jesus. Secondly, the prefix "co" (coming from the Latin prefix "cum") *does not mean "equal"* but rather "with." If "co" meant equal, then St. Paul would have been referring to all Christians as equal to God when he called Christians God's "co-workers." Didn't happen. That would be blasphemy. Not what St. Paul meant.

St. Paul meant "working with," and the same applies to the prefix "co" and the word "redeemer" when referring to Mary.

The Latin suffix "trix" simply refers to a female. The verb "to redeem" (*redimere* in Latin) means to "buy back."

Okay, let's now put this word back together. The "co-redemptrix" term simply means "*a woman with the Redeemer*" or literally "a woman who buys back with." And the "with" refers to "Jesus."

So, now that we know what the title "co-redemptrix" means, let's see if this title accurately describes the role of the Mother of Jesus as the "woman with the Redeemer" more than any other woman (or man for that matter) in human history.

Mary Co-redemptrix in the Bible

The Bible says that we have all been saved or "sanctified" by the "offering of the body of Jesus, once for all" (Heb 10:10).

Now, precisely from whom did Jesus get the instrument of Redemption? He received his body from Mary.

Now, that's unique and unrepeatable in terms of cooperating with the Redeemer of the world: giving the Redeemer his body, which becomes the very instrument of Redemption!

I remember a very blessed experience of spending three days with Mother Teresa in Calcutta, India, during which time I asked her the question point blank: "Mother, do you believe Mary is the Co-redemptrix with Jesus?" She immediately responded, "Of course, Mary is the Co-redemptrix! She gave Jesus his body, and the body of Jesus is what saved us!" I then responded, "Mother, that's the difference between saints and theologians — you just said in five seconds what it takes us books to write!"

Point number two regarding Mary's unique right to be called "Co-redemptrix": *her unparalleled suffering with Jesus, from the moment of the Annunciation until its climactic conclusion at Calvary.*

Mary knew (as a devout Jewish woman knowledgeable in Old Testament Scripture would know) that the coming Messiah would have much to suffer, as was prophesied by prophets like Isaiah.[30] From the moment of her "yes," Mary would realize that *her Son would be born to die.* This realization would remain in her motherly mind and heart from the moment of her "yes" until its frightening fulfillment on the Cross.

The Bible also confirms Mary's special role of suffering with Jesus in his saving work. When Mary and Joseph presented the Infant Jesus in the Temple to offer him to the Lord (as was Jewish custom), the prophet Simeon stepped forward and identified Jesus as the "Light of the world" and as a "sign of contradiction" for the world. Simeon then turned to Mary and prophesied, "[A]nd your heart, too, will be pierced" (Lk 2:35).

Simple summary of Simeon's words: "You, Mary, are the Mother of the Sign of Contradiction who will suffer for the world's salvation. Therefore, *you, too, will suffer.*" What's difficult to understand about the fact that if a Child is called to suffer, that Child's mother is also called to suffer? Every parent would nod his or her head "yes" to this obvious parental reality.

A few years back, a father called into a live radio program I was having on this subject of Mary as Co-redemptrix. He jumped into the conversation: "I don't understand all the controversy about calling Mary the 'Co-redemptrix.' My daughter just had a life-threatening operation, and I had to wait in the waiting room until the operation was over. I can tell you, it would have been much easier for me as a parent to be on the operating table than to be in the waiting room. If a child suffers, the parent suffers. I can only imagine the sufferings in Mary's heart as she was watching her Son die on the Cross during that horrible torture. What's the big deal in calling her Co-redemptrix with Jesus? That's just common sense."

Let's move on to Golgotha, the place where Jesus is crucified and where Mary's suffering with the Redeemer reaches its crescendo.

Now, Christian writers down through the ages have sought to capture the depth of the suffering of this immaculate mother at the foot of the Cross in everything from liturgical hymns such as the *"Stabat Mater"* (the "Mother Standing") from the 15th century, down to the words of St. Pope John Paul II, who said that Mary at Calvary was "spiritually crucified with her crucified son."[31]

But let's try something a bit more personal. I'd like you to think of the person in the world that you love the most. If it's a close battle between two people (like Mom or Dad), then just choose one or the other — it'll serve our example fine.

So, you have that one person in mind, right? Okay, then, I want you to imagine a group of strangers coming up to the person you love the most, and these strangers take your beloved, bind his or her hands with rope or a chain, and take him or her away to the local authorities while continually slapping, hitting, mocking, and spitting on your loved one along the way.

Then, the local authorities unjustly sentence your completely innocent loved one to being lashed in public. (Keep the focus here on your loved one — not on anyone else.) They tie your loved one to a column and start whipping this person repeatedly, over and over, with whips that have bone or rock attached to the ends, tearing pieces of flesh out of your loved one's body with each stroke. This person is now terribly bloody all over, is almost killed by this torturous attack, and you, for your part, can only watch.

Now, as if that weren't enough (I know you're making the association, but hang with this just a little longer — keep focusing on your personal loved one), your tortured beloved is then crowned with two-to-three-inch-long thorns all over his or her skull, is forced to carry a weight of more than a hundred pounds on his or her shoulder up a long hill, and falls in exhaustion three times. Finally, your loved one is brutally executed at a public crucifixion (keep picturing in your mind your most loved person) and is hanging on that cross. The crowd is yelling the most terrible things about your beloved, even though they know nothing about this person. You are right in front of him or her, watching, crying, and trying to console your loved one, at least by your presence. This lasts for three hours, and then, finally, your loved one dies.

Now, during this entire horrible event, you have done nothing other than watch your loved one experience this terrible evil. Why haven't you done anything but watch? Why haven't you tried to stop it? Why didn't you defend your loved one to the people in the crowds saying such terrible things, which you knew were absolutely untrue?

Because God told you not to. God told you, instead, to patiently endure it and to offer these sufferings to God to be used precisely to save other human souls, including the needy people who just tortured and killed your beloved.

This is the story of Mary Co-redemptrix, and there was no imagining in her story. It all really happened.

As certain Popes have taught, Jesus was the Person she loved most in the world. I believe she was told by God to endure this untold suffering and to offer the sufferings of her heart in union with the sufferings of his body for the salvation of all humanity.

Mary "died with Jesus in her heart,"[32] and Mary "redeemed the human race together with Christ."[33] But this co-redeeming and co-dying is always in the context of Jesus being the only divine Redeemer and Mary's role being absolutely and entirely dependent on Jesus. "Co" does not mean equal!

The very first theological idea that the early Christians had about Mary, after recognizing her as the Mother of

Jesus, was that she fulfilled the role of becoming the "New Eve"[34] with Jesus, the "New Adam."

These early Christian writers rightly understood that just as Eve, through her disobedience, was instrumental with Adam in committing the Original Sin and its resulting loss of grace for the human family, so Mary, through her obedience, became the New Eve who uniquely cooperated with Jesus (whom St. Paul calls the "New Adam") in bringing back grace to the human family.

Now listen to these words of the "contemporary master" on Mary as Co-redemptrix, St. Pope John Paul II:

> Crucified spiritually with her crucified Son, [Mary] contemplated with heroic love the death of her God, she lovingly consented to the "immolation of this victim which she herself had brought forth"[35]...
> In fact, Mary's role as Co-redemptrix did not cease with the glorification of her Son.[36]

Saint John Paul is saying that Mary consented to the sufferings of Jesus, as well as to her own sufferings, for our sake, and thus, through her joint suffering with Jesus, becomes our spiritual mother.

Isn't it true that the first thing a mother does for her child is to suffer — for some mothers, almost from the moment of their child's conception? So it is for Mary, who suffers to give "spiritual birth" to all who desire it at Calvary.

But what does John Paul mean when he says that "Mary's role as Co-redemptrix did not cease with the glorification of her son?" This "glorification" part refers to Jesus dying on the Cross. So the further question is this:

"How does Mary's role as Co-redemptrix continue after Jesus' death at Calvary?"

Well, as we have said, Mary uniquely shared in Jesus' saving work of Redemption. *Mary alone* participated in the actual obtaining of the graces of salvation with Jesus as the Co-redemptrix working and suffering with the Redeemer to restore graces to the world.

But once these saving graces have been *obtained*, they still must be *dispensed*. So, at this point, Mary's role as Co-redemptrix with Jesus, the Redeemer, must now continue as Mary's role as Mediatrix with Jesus, the Mediator.

Chapter 8

Who Mediated the Mediator?

One day while sitting around the dinner table, one of my eight children asked me, "Dad, what do the words 'Co-redemptrix, Mediatrix, and Advocate' mean?" Granted, that's not the usual kind of question you get for conversation at a family dinner, but the kids knew that I had been working on an international movement and previous book with those words as its title. (Okay, I'll fess up — it's even abbreviated on my license plate!) I was stumped for a moment. It's one thing to use the typical theological jargon to explain these Marian titles, but there were eight kids looking up at their father (not their professor) and expecting an answer that they could understand.

Suddenly in the midst of this domestic darkness, a light bulb went off in my little brain (I'm assuming from above), and I calmly and comfortably responded: "Well, kids, it's like any mother. What are the three things that all good mothers do for their children? Number one, they *suffer* for their children, and not just in giving birth, but throughout the mother's entire life. Number two, they *nourish* their children, not just with food, but with love and formation throughout their children's lives. Number three, they *plead* for their children, interceding for what's best for their children, whether it's at school, on the sports field, or even sometimes while they're at college and beyond.

"Well, kids, that's what the Blessed Mother does for us, but it's with sanctifying grace — the grace that saves us and makes us holy. The Blessed Mother suffered with Jesus to get this grace for us — that's what Co-redemptrix means. She then distributes the grace of salvation with Jesus — that's what Mediatrix of all graces means. Finally, she pleads for our needs before Jesus — that's what Advocate means."

Concluding this seemingly brilliant analogy, I settled back in my chair at the head of the table with great self-pleasure, only to realize that half the brood were utterly sidetracked through side conversations, while the other half were focused on the purgative duty of finishing the peas.

Still, I think there's something worthwhile to this domestic example because, while few may feel immediately comfortable with a title like a "Mediatrix," all should feel comfortable and have a natural aptitude to understanding the loving actions of a *good mother* — one who generously nourishes and forms her children in the natural order of human life. That's what Mary does, but on the supernatural level of human life as the *"Mediatrix of all graces."*

Jesus, the One Mediator and Mary, Mediatrix

Based on nearly two millennia of Christian Tradition and teaching, the Popes have consistently taught that after Mary uniquely participated in obtaining the graces of Redemption as Co-redemptrix with the Redeemer, she then continued her role of motherly intercession by *distributing* the graces of redemption as Mediatrix of all graces with Jesus, the one divine Mediator.

As always, Mary's human roles are absolutely dependent on Jesus' divine roles — she participates as a human in what Jesus does as God. Don't all Christians do a similar thing when we participate in the divine life of Jesus through faith and Baptism?

Here's the repeating equation: His divine action, our human participation.

But what about the verse in the Bible that states Jesus is the "one mediator between God and man"? The verse, in context, states that "there is one mediator between God and man, the man Christ Jesus" (1 Tim 2:5). Saint Pope John Paul II tells us that what St. Paul is condemning here is any type of mediation that is "competing" or "parallel" to that of Jesus Christ in reaching the Heavenly Father. But St. Paul is in no way speaking against a participation, a cooperation, a sharing in the one perfect mediation of Jesus by human beings. In fact, this first letter of Timothy begins with St. Paul asking for Christians to "pray" and "supplicate" (or intercede) for one another. Is praying and interceding for another person not a form of mediation?

The Bible is full of instances where God has ordained human beings to be "secondary mediators" between himself and his people. For example, the great patriarchs of the Old Testament (Abraham, Isaac, Jacob, Moses, etc.) are all human beings whom God directly appointed to be mediators of a covenant (a sacred promise and union) between God and the People of Israel. The prophets of the Old Testament are another example of

God-appointed mediators of communication between God and His people. And let's not forget the glorious angels, those marvelous spiritual persons who are constantly mediating between God and humanity in both the Old and New Testaments in an effort to unite God and the human family.

That's really what a mediator is. A mediator (taken from the Greek word "*mesitis,*" which literally means a "go-between") is a person or persons who intervene between two parties for the sake of *unifying* and *reconciling* those two parties.

Sometimes we have the opposite idea of mediators. We can have the idea that if someone is a "go-between" between you and another individual, this means you have to physically move farther way from each other so the mediator can get between you and the other person. Well, the complete opposite is true of *spiritual mediation.*

Spiritual mediation doesn't require you to move farther away from the one you seek to be united with because of the mediator. On the contrary, in spiritual mediation, the person intercedes for your spiritual union without causing you to take one step, either physically or spiritually, away from the one you desire to be united with. It all happens spiritually — in the order of grace and in the domain of the heart.

Simply put, a true spiritual mediator accomplishes reconciliation and union with you and the person you seek to be united with through the power of God's grace.

This is why Mary can rightly be called our "Mediatrix" with Jesus. She intercedes to unite us, her later children, with Jesus, her first-born Child, by dispensing the graces of the Redemption to our hearts.

Because Jesus, who is the "First Uncreated Grace," entered the world through the intercession of Mary, we shouldn't be too surprised that Jesus would arrange it so all sanctifying grace obtained from his sacrifice on Calvary would also come to us through the intercession of Mary.

First of all, then, Mary is called the Mediatrix of all graces because she mediated Jesus himself to us, who is the source of all grace. In fact, it is true to say that *Mary as Mediatrix actually mediated Jesus, the one Mediator, to us!* Her free, feminine, and faithful "yes" to God's invitation is what mediated to the world our one divine Mediator. For this, all Christians (at least) must rejoice and thank Mary! Mary Mediatrix mediated the Mediator.

The Mediatrix at Cana

Mary's motherly mediation in the order of grace continues long after the Annunciation. At the biblical account of the wedding of Cana, the Mother of Jesus notices that the wine has run out, a major gap in hospitality for the wedding couple and, potentially, a huge source of social embarrassment.

Mary goes to Jesus in an act of direct, purposeful intercession for the wedding couple and asks him to perform a miracle to create more wine. Jesus does so, and the attendants comment on how unusual it is to save the best wine for last (see Jn 2:1-10).

This Cana passage is packed with important meaning and symbolism for our topic. First, Jesus responds to Mary's statement "They have no wine" with the response, "Woman, what is this to me and to you? My hour has not yet come" (Jn 2:4). When Jesus calls Mary "Woman," he is, once again, identifying her as *the Woman of Scripture*, the Woman of Genesis to the Woman of Revelation, who will be Jesus' single greatest companion in the mission of saving the human race. His statement "My hour has not yet come" refers to the "hour" of the crucifixion at Calvary. As the famous radio and television personality of the fifties and sixties Archbishop Fulton Sheen once paraphrased this passage, Jesus is saying to Mary: "What is this to us — us, two, who are on this joint mission of salvation? If I perform this miracle, we are on the fast track from Cana to Calvary, for everyone will then publicly know who I am, and that will eventually lead to my crucifixion. Are you, Woman, ready for this?"

That's why Mary's response is so profound. She responds in faith to Jesus by telling the servants (in her last and perennially appropriate words of the Bible), *"Do whatever he tells you"* (Jn 2:5).

Jesus performed the miracle in answer to the loving intercession of Mary for the wedding couple, who, by the way, were not known to be disciples of Jesus. More symbolism here: Mary's role as Mediatrix is not restricted to Christian "disciples" of Jesus but is active for *all humanity* in the variety of our wants and needs.

Who would have thought that Jesus, God made man, would announce his public ministry over something as mundane as a second round of wine at a wedding? Still more symbolism: Mary cares about the most seemingly mundane needs of our lives as well, and she will be quick to bring them to the attention of Jesus — if we ask her.

The Mediatrix at Calvary

It's also important to always remember, once again, that we understand that Mary's role as Mediatrix of all graces comes as an appropriate result of her role as Co-redemptrix. It's because Mary suffered with and under Jesus to obtain grace that she is appropriately assigned by Jesus to dispense the graces.

Again, the brilliance of St. John Paul II lends light to this role of Mary. The great Marian Pope tells us that Mary's role as "Mediatrix" is "intrinsic to" or already contained within "her role as Mother."[37] To be a spiritual mother is to be a mediatrix of grace. For mothers to be mothers, they must be able to nourish their children — so, too, in the life of grace in our relationship with Mary.

This is why we can understand the words of Jesus from the Cross "Behold, your mother" to also mean, "Behold, your mediatrix."

In sum: Mary is Mediatrix of all graces because she was Co-redemptrix with Jesus in acquiring the graces. That's why her role as Mediatrix of all the graces obtained at Calvary by Jesus and, secondarily by she herself, isn't arbitrary. It's not by chance — it's by sacrifice.

On the historic day of February 11, 2013, when Pope Benedict XVI announced to the world his surprising resignation, he also published a letter in which he invoked Mary as the "Mediatrix of all graces."[38] This statement by then Pope Benedict just continues centuries of official teachings that Mary mediates to the fallen human race every grace necessary for our salvation.

But Christians have been calling Mary the "Mediatrix" in thousands of Christian writings that go back to the first centuries since Jesus walked the earth.[39] This shouldn't surprise us. Mary's motherly mediation actually goes back to the first moment of the New Testament when the young Virgin of Nazareth does what no other creature does — she mediates Jesus, the One Mediator, for the salvation of the whole world.

Chapter 9

'Did You Call Mary a Lawyer?'

Some years back, I was giving a presentation in Bolivia to a group of Latin American representatives of various Marian organizations during which I referred to Mary's role as Advocate, which in Spanish is "*Abogada.*" Now, *abogada* is also the word used in Latin America for "lawyer."

After the talk, two women representatives of Latin American countries came up to me with concerned expressions on their faces. One woman began, "Did we hear you correctly? Did you call Mary a 'lawyer?'" I responded: "Well, in a certain sense, Mary is a lawyer as one who speaks on our behalf [the meaning of 'advocate'], but it's a different kind of court. It's the court of Christ the King, and we are her clients. Mary is our Advocate, speaking on our behalf."

Well, this seemed to satisfy the two women representatives. Two weeks later, I was giving a similar presentation in Dallas, Texas, and when the time in the presentation came to discuss the Mother of Jesus as "Advocate," I recounted what had just happened down in Bolivia with the two representatives. After the talk, a stately, gray-haired gentleman walked up to the podium and said, with a particularly strong Texas accent: "Son, in all my years as a Texas lawyer, I've never been compared to the Blessed Mother. Here's a $1,000 donation for your Marian movement." That's the way one Texas lawyer showed his appreciation for the Marian title of Advocate!

"Advocate" is probably Mary's most ancient title. In the second century, the French (then Gallic) Church Father St. Irenaeus called Mary an "advocate" or intercessor to plead for the salvation of Eve. Quite the historic twist — the New Eve interceding for the Old Eve!

Yes, the term "advocate" means "one who speaks on behalf of someone else." Short form: an intercessor. And Christians have believed since the first centuries of Christian faith that Mary is the major intercessor on behalf of humanity to Jesus, who is and will always be the King in the Kingdom of God.

In the Old Testament, there was a fascinating role for the mother of each of the kings in the line of the great King David. The mother of the king was given the official role and title of "Queen Mother" (*"Gebirah"* in Hebrew, which literally means the "Great Lady"). This role was granted to the king's mother and not to the king's wives (which, incidentally, avoided great domestic disputes — King Solomon, for example, had 700 wives!).

The Queen Mother had more than just an honorary role in the Jewish Kingdom. She had a key position in service to the king and to the kingdom: the Queen Mother was the principal *advocate* for the people to the king. If a common person wanted to bring something to the attention of the king, he wouldn't dare approach the king directly. Rather, he would approach the Queen Mother and ask her to bring the matter to the king's attention. All the members of the Jewish Kingdom knew full well of the Queen Mother's intercessory power as their potential advocate before the king.

In fact, the Bible records the extraordinary intercessory power of the Queen Mother as well as the docile disposition of the king to quickly grant his mother's pleas. For example, when Bathsheba, the Queen Mother, goes before her son, King Solomon, Scripture records that the King bowed to her (while all the King's wives bowed to him). Also, King Solomon had a throne brought to his right side for the Queen Mother (the position of honor) and publicly declared: "Make your request, my mother. For I will not refuse you"(1 Kgs 2:19). That's an office of unequaled intercessory power within the entire Kingdom of Israel.

Well, in the New Testament, we receive a new "King of Kings" and, therefore, also a new "Queen Mother." When the Archangel Gabriel comes to Mary with his heavenly invitation, he uses "royal" terms and images to convey to the young Virgin that her future Son will become the "King" in the line of David: "He will be great, and will be called the Son of the Most High; and the Lord God will give him the throne of his father, David. He will reign over the House of Jacob forever; and of his kingdom, there will be no end" (Lk 1:32-33).

Notice all those "king" and "kingdom" references? That's because Jesus would indeed become the new and everlasting King, not only of the Kingdom of David, but of the universal Kingdom of all creation.

Well, with a new King, you also have a new "Queen Mother."

By virtue of being mother of the King of Kings, Mary immediately becomes the new Queen Mother, the new *Gebirah*, the new "Great Lady." And Mary's role as the new Queen Mother in the Kingdom of God carries the same responsibility: She will now be the principal intercessor on behalf of the people of the Kingdom to Jesus, King of the Kingdom.

How far does Mary's intercessory role as Queen and Advocate extend? As far as the Kingdom of Jesus extends — it is universal and all-inclusive.

We see Mary's role as Advocate at the Wedding of Cana, where she powerfully and effectively intercedes to Jesus for the needs of the wedding couple (see Jn 2:1-10).

We see Mary crowned as "Queen and Advocate" in the Book of Revelation as the "woman clothed with the sun with the moon under her feet and on her head a crown of twelve stars" (Rev 12:1). Yes, this "Queen Mother" crowned in the Book of Revelation is Mary, for she gave "birth to a male child, one who is to rule the nations with an iron rod" (Rev 12:5). The woman must be Mary, because *only Mary* gave birth to the "male child" who would be the universal King and Ruler.

Yes, the Queen of Jesus' Kingdom will be Advocate for all the subjects of the Kingdom, bringing their needs, yours and mine, to the attention of our King.

How appropriate it is, then, that the early Christians would see Mary as their Queen and Advocate interceding for them.

One of the most ancient prayers to Mary illustrates this early Church confidence in the intercessory power of their Queen and Advocate. It goes by the title *Sub Tuum Praesiduum* ("Under Your Protection") and dates back to the middle of the third century:

We fly to your patronage, O Holy Mother of God.
Despise not our petitions in our necessities,

but deliver us from all dangers,
O ever glorious and blessed Virgin.

We can see why Christian writers have called Mary the "Advocate" throughout the ages. In the well-known 12th century Christian prayer "Hail, Holy Queen," Mary is invoked, "Turn then, O most gracious Advocate, your eyes of mercy toward us ... ."

Try to visualize Mary's service to Jesus and to us as a type of circle. Picture a circle with Jesus at the top of the circle and us, the human family, at the bottom. At the top of the circle, visualize Mary's role as the Co-redemptrix next to Jesus at Calvary as she participated in obtaining the graces of salvation. Now, going down the left side of the circle, envision Mary's role as the Mediatrix of all graces, bringing down the graces of Jesus to us at the bottom of the circle. Finally, at the bottom of the circle, Mary as Advocate takes our needs, the pleas and petitions of the human family, and brings them back up to the top of the circle, presenting them with love at the Throne of Jesus, our King.

This is the circle of Mary's motherly, loving intercession: at once, serving Jesus and at the same time, serving us.

Chapter 10

A 'New Marian Dogma' in World News?

W hat's been in the secular news about Mary should certainly be known by intelligent and educated Christians and non-Christians, too.

Newsweek, the BBC, National Public Radio, *The New York Times* — these world renowned secular news agencies and many more have all covered the movement in the Catholic Church for a possible "fifth Marian Dogma" regarding Mary. What is this movement about, and why is the secular world so interested in it?

Almost 100 years ago, a well-known Catholic cardinal from Belgium, Cardinal Désiré Mercier, started a petition drive in the Catholic Church to request the Pope at the time (Pope Benedict XV) to pronounce a fifth "dogma" or solemn definition that the Virgin Mary is the Spiritual Mother of all humanity (in specific terms, the "Mediatrix of All Graces"). Mercier gathered several hundred petitions from Catholic bishops at the time and presented them to Pope Benedict XV.

A few years later, a certain Polish priest, Fr. Maximilian Kolbe, joined in this Catholic petition drive through his international Marian apostolate known as the "Army of the Immaculate." Father Maximilian Kolbe later became

St. Maximilian Kolbe as he heroically offered his life in exchange for the life of a married man in the Auschwitz death camp during World War II.

The petition movement for this fifth Marian Dogma of Mary's Spiritual Motherhood soon spread worldwide. Millions of petitions have been sent to the Popes of the 20th and 21st centuries to encourage them to make this infallible statement about Mary as our Spiritual Mother.

By the way, there's nothing new here with the petition drive. A large and lengthy petition drive encouraged Blessed Pope Pius IX to declare the dogma of the Immaculate Conception back in 1854. The same holds true for Venerable Pope Pius XII who declared the Dogma of Mary's Assumption into heaven in 1950 after the Holy See received millions of petitions over the course of 95 years. In fact, both Popes thanked the Christian faithful who had sent in those petitions, as they helped the Pope to discern that it was, in fact, the "right time" for these Marian dogmas.

Another word here about petition drives in the Catholic Church. Sometimes the wrong idea can be drawn from these drives, as if the people are *demanding* on some democratic basis that the Pope do a certain thing. Or sometimes a given petition being circulated is asking the Pope to change something beyond his power or against the doctrine of Jesus and the Church. Neither of the above are authentic Catholic petition drives.

An authentic Catholic petition drive is where the members of the Church *respectfully and humbly* write to the Pope for the purpose of letting him know something dear to their hearts — something they deem important for the Church at a given time. But it's not a demand. It can't call for a change in doctrine. And it's not pressure. It's a request made in love and with *full respect and obedience* to the Pope's final decision.

In fact, the canon law of the Church calls it a Christian "duty" to bring to the mind of the pastors of the Church something the faithful believe to be for the good of the Church.[40]

Back to this movement for the Fifth Marian Dogma. Just in the last 15 years, more than 8 million petitions from 168 countries have been sent to the Vatican for the papal definition of Mary's Spiritual Motherhood. More than 500 cardinals and bishops have also sent in their petitions to the recent Popes to encourage them to make this Marian proclamation. (And these are the numbers just for the last 15 years — only the Vatican would know the numbers for almost the last hundred years!) That makes this movement for Mary's spiritual maternity the largest annual petition drive in the history of the Catholic Church.[41]

But it's not just numbers. It's grace! Yes, grace.

Each time in history when a Pope has solemnly declared a dogma about Jesus' Mother, one could argue that *historic graces have been poured down upon the Church and the world.*

Take, for example, the Dogma of the Immaculate Conception.

The historical situation for the Church at the time was pretty rough. In 1848, a secular military force had come up from southern Italy, forcefully taken over the Vatican, and sought the death of Pope Pius IX. He was able to sneak out of the Vatican and make his way out of Rome in disguise.

Pius IX went into exile in Gaeta, Italy. The secular commentary on the streets in Rome was that the Catholic

Church was now over and had run its course, just like the Roman Empire had previously done. Things looked bleak.

While in exile, two cardinals approached Pius IX and essentially said to him: "Holy Father, our only way to return to Rome and safeguard the Church is to proclaim the Dogma of the Immaculate Conception. Let Our Lady intercede on our behalf and that of the Church."[42] With this intervention, along with the millions of petitions he had already received from the faithful worldwide, Pius IX decided to turn to Mary. While still in exile in 1849, he wrote to every bishop in the world, declaring his intention to proclaim the Dogma of the Immaculate Conception.

History reveals the outcome. The Dogma of the Immaculate Conception was proclaimed in 1854. Pope Pius IX returned to the Vatican. The papacy was renewed and strengthened through this Dogma and the later declaration of Papal Infallibility by the same Pope at the First Vatican Council in 1870. The Church was revitalized in unity and fidelity under the fortified and saintly pontificate of Blessed Pius IX.

So, I'd argue that when a Marian dogma happens, *grace happens.*

Many contemporary commentators, including the late Mother Teresa, Mother Angelica, founder of the Eternal Word Television Network (or "EWTN"), hundreds of cardinals and bishops, and millions of Catholics and non-Catholics alike believe that the Church and the whole world would greatly benefit through the proclamation of a new Dogma of Mary's Spiritual Motherhood today.

But why would a proclamation by the Pope make such a difference in the world?

For the simple reason that *Mary's titles are her functions.* In other words, the three titles of Co-redemptrix,

Mediatrix, and Advocate are actually action steps of grace and intercession Mary can fully activate on behalf of humanity — but only if we give Mary our free consent, our "yes."

That's exactly what a proclamation from the Pope as the Church's highest authority would signify: a "yes" from humanity's highest and greatest spiritual representative to activate Mary's full intercessory power.

God will not allow Mary (or anybody else for that matter) to force grace upon us against our will. We have to be open to it. We have to consent to God's help.

And that's the purpose and the power of the papal proclamation of the Dogma of Mary Co-redemptrix, Mediatrix of all graces, and Advocate. It is the Pope's "yes" on behalf of us all to accept the great abundance of historic graces that God wishes to pour out on the world at this important time in human history.

But don't just take my word for it. Take Mary's.

From 1945 to 1959, the Mother of Jesus appeared under the title of "The Lady of All Nations" in Amsterdam, Holland, to a Dutch woman, Ida Peerdeman, and revealed extraordinary messages about challenging future events and heaven's remedy. These Marian apparitions and messages were declared by the local Church authority as being of an authentic "supernatural origin" on May 31, 2002.[43]

Our Lady began appearing to Ida on March 25, 1945, during World II, and rightly predicted the end of the war in Holland in May of that same year. Along with messages calling for a return to Jesus and his Cross, the Lady also made a number of prophecies about political events as a sign to the world, upon their fulfillment, of the apparition's authenticity.

Here are just a few examples of the many fulfilled social and political predictions contained in this Marian message (as noted by political historian Dr. Richard Russell):

1. In 1945, a prophecy of the return of a state of Israel (fulfilled in 1948);
2. Another 1945 prophecy of "China with a red flag" (fulfilled in 1949 with the Communist revolution);
3. A 1949 vision of Korea with a line splitting the country in two (fulfilled in 1950 with the Korean War, leading to North and South Korea);
4. A 1947 vision of conflict in Cairo, with the prophecy of much division between nations as a result (seems to have been fulfilled in February 2011 with the "Arab Spring Revolt").

This brief sampling doesn't include a number of other social and economic prophecies, such as a grave global crisis in the economy, the modern attack on religion and moral values, and the unprecedented natural disasters that have all proved true in our day.

Why would the Lady of All Nations reveal secular predictions concerning social, economic, and geo-political events? It's heaven's way of providing a sign to the Church and to the world that these messages are not of a human but, rather, of a supernatural origin — and thereby, they also offer a supernatural solution for the serious global problems in our day.

She did all this precisely to get the attention *and the credence* of the secular world, so we will all listen with an open heart to Our Lady's spiritual remedy for the "degeneration, disaster, and war" that make up the major headlines of our day. One former American CIA Agent put it this way: "That Dutch woman knew more about future social and political events than the knowledge of the U.S. Central Intelligence Agency and the Russian KGB combined! This information couldn't have just come from her."[44]

The "backbone" message of the Lady of All Nations is her repeated and consistent request *for the Pope to declare Mary's roles of Co-redemptrix, Mediatrix, and Advocate as a "new Marian dogma."* In fact, the Lady of All Nations confirms over and over again that *the proclamation of this Marian dogma is the condition and remedy to bring peace to the entire world.*

In these Marian messages from Amsterdam, the Mother of Jesus states that through the proclamation of this fifth Marian dogma, she will be able to intercede to obtain the "grace, redemption, and peace" that will overcome the "degeneration, disaster, and war" that presently dominate the headlines of today's world.

For example, the Lady of All Nations strongly directs us: "Work and ask for the Dogma ... you must petition the Holy Father for this Dogma ... once the Dogma has been proclaimed, then the Lady of All Nations will bring peace, *true peace* to the world."[45]

Let's get to a few excerpts from some of the Amsterdam messages that focus on Our Lady's *remedies for today.*

On February 11, 1951, the Lady of All Nations revealed to Ida a prayer that she asked the entire world to pray. It is a prayer asking Jesus to send down the Holy Spirit into the "hearts" of all nations precisely to prevent the moral decay, natural disasters, and wars and rumors of wars so prevalent throughout the world. Here are Our Lady's specific words as reported by the visionary:

> "Let all men return to the Cross! Only this can bring peace and tranquility." I am still standing in front of the Cross with the Lady. She says to me, "Repeat this after me. Do say this prayer in front of the Cross":

> > "Lord Jesus Christ, Son of the Father, send now Your Spirit over the earth. Let the Holy Spirit live in the hearts of all nations, that they may be preserved from degeneration, disasters, and war. May the Lady of All Nations, the Blessed Virgin Mary, be our Advocate, Amen."[46]

I am still standing in front of the Cross and have said the prayer and repeated the Lady's words phrase by phrase. Now I see them written in large characters.

The Lady continues, "My child, this prayer is so short and simple that each one can say it in his own tongue, before his own crucifix; and those who have no crucifix, repeat it to themselves. This is the message which I have come to give you today, for I have *now* come to tell you that I *want* to *save* souls. Let all men cooperate in this great work for the world!

Note how the Lady says that this prayer is "so short and simple" that all can pray it. Succinct, but powerful! In another message, she reiterates that this prayer holds great power before the throne of God and that "whoever" you are, you are invited to pray it.[47] The messages further specify that this prayer should be prayed precisely to prepare the way for the proclamation of the dogma of Mary Co-Redemptrix, Mediatrix, and Advocate.[48]

During her April 29, 1951, message, Mary gives her own explanation of this new Marian dogma and assures us that, though there will be controversy regarding its proclamation, its victorious outcome is "already assured":

"I stand here as the Co-Redemptrix and Advocate. Everything should be concentrated on that. Repeat this after me: The new dogma will be the 'dogma of the Co-Redemptrix.' Notice, I lay special emphasis on the 'Co.' I have said that it will arouse much controversy. Once again I tell you that the Church, 'Rome,' will carry it through and silence all objections. The Church, 'Rome,' will become stronger and mightier in proportion to the resistance she puts up in the struggle.

"My purpose and my commission to you is none other than to urge the Church, the theologians, to wage this battle. For the Father, the Son, and the Holy Spirit will to send the Lady, chosen to bear the Redeemer, into *this* world, as Co-Redemptrix and Advocate. I have said, 'This time is our time.' By this I mean the following: The world is caught up in degeneration and superficiality. It is at a loss. Therefore, the Father sends me to be the Advocate, to implore the Holy Spirit to come. For the world is not saved by force, the world will be saved by the Spirit.

"In the sufferings, both spiritual and bodily, the Lady, the Mother, has shared. She has always gone before. As soon as the Father had elected her, she was the Co-Redemptrix with the Redeemer, who came into the world as the Man-God. Tell that to your theologians.

"I know well, the struggle will be hard and bitter" (and then the Lady smiles to herself and seems to gaze into the far distance), "*but the outcome is already assured.*"

Great encouragement here! Along with the crucial importance of our ongoing prayers and petitions for this fifth Marian Dogma that the Lady of All Nations specifically requests, we also have Our Lady's assurance that this dogma will be! And this Mother does not break her promises.

The single most important message from the Lady of All Nations comes on May 31, 1954, which, at that time, was the feast of Mary as the Mediatrix of all graces. Here, Our Lady reveals to us the imperative to "Pray and ask for this dogma … . You must petition the Holy Father for the dogma." She also gives Ida a vision of its future fulfillment in St. Peter's Basilica:

"Once more I am here — the Co-Redemptrix, Mediatrix, and Advocate is now standing before you. Theologians and apostles of the Lord Jesus Christ, listen carefully: I have given you the explanation of the dogma. Work and ask for this dogma. You must petition the Holy Father for this dogma.

All of a sudden, it is as if I was standing with the Lady over the dome of a big church and as we enter, I hear the Lady say, 'I am taking you inside this. Tell others what I let you see and hear." *We* are now in a very big church, in St. Peter's. I see lots of cardinals and bishops. The Pope enters. ... People applaud. The choir begins to sing. Now the Holy Father is announcing something, while holding up two fingers. Then all at once the Lady is standing on the globe again and says with a smile, "In this way, my child, I have let you see what is the Will of the Lord Jesus Christ. This day will in due time be the 'Coronation Day' of his Mother, the 'Lady of All Nations'."

In the same May 31, 1954, message, Our Lady also refers to the proclamation of this dogma as the ultimate fulfillment of Mary's own self-prophecy in the Bible: "My prophecy, 'From henceforth all generations shall call me blessed,' will be fulfilled more than ever before, once the dogma has been proclaimed."

Toward the end of this message, the Lady of All Nations reveals that *only with the proclamation of the new dogma of Mary Co-Redemptrix, Mediatrix, and Advocate will she be able to bring "peace, true peace, to the world"*:

"'The Lady of All Nations' desires unity in the Holy Spirit of Truth. The world is encompassed by a false spirit — *Satan.* When the dogma, the last dogma in Marian history, has been proclaimed, 'the Lady of All Nations' will give *peace, true peace* to the world. The nations, however, must say my prayer in union with the Church. They must know that 'the Lady of All Nations' has come as Co-Redemptrix, Mediatrix, and Advocate. So be it!"

It really doesn't sound like too much for Our Lady to ask: a daily praying of the Prayer of the Lady of All Nations and the sending of a petition to the Pope (a love letter of support and encouragement, not a pressuring letter of political lobby!) for him to proclaim the dogma of Mary as Co-redemptrix, Mediatrix, and Advocate. The promised fruit is nothing short of true world peace.

Once again, her titles are her functions, and she awaits our "yes" to activate her titles completely on our behalf.

All people are free to incorporate what our Mother asked us to do. We can pray the Prayer of the Lady of All Nations each day. We can write a letter to Pope Francis (in love and respect) and ask him to prayerfully consider proclaiming this dogma as Our Lady asks. (By the way, the Pope's address is an easy one: Pope Francis, 00120 Vatican City.)

We can all participate by responding to the challenging world headlines of today in the Marian way, with a new and historic release of the grace and peace of Jesus, through Mary's maternal and powerful intercession.

The world needs its Mother. What are we waiting for?

Chapter 11

'Why Is Mary Appearing All Over the Place?'

A reporter from a major secular newspaper called me one day and asked, "Why is Mary appearing all over the place? Why so many apparitions at one time? Is this a good sign or a bad sign?"

I answered, "Those are questions that call for distinctions.

"First, Mary is the Spiritual Mother of All Peoples. Of course, the Mother of Jesus would come to all parts of the world, to all continents, with her motherly message of a return to Jesus and his Gospel.

"Second, we should thank God that he is sending Jesus' Mother down from heaven with these extraordinary graces of conversion, healing, and other miracles to move our hearts back to Jesus and the Church. Thank God for his generosity, as these Marian apparitions over the course of the last 150 years or so have resulted in millions of conversions to and back to the Church.

"Third, if we keep in mind the reason for private revelation, it's a sign that we, as a human family, need more encouragement to live the Gospel of Jesus. Private revelation has as its purpose not to replace the Gospel but to return people to the faithful living out of the Gospel. If the Mother of God is coming today in what constitutes more Church-approved apparitions than in any other age in human history, this also tells us that we must not be doing so well in living the Truth of Jesus and his Church. Otherwise, we wouldn't need so many reminders from our Spiritual Mother. She's not coming down because she's bored in heaven. She's coming down because our world needs it."

That, in a nutshell, is the nature and purpose of private revelation — not to reveal new doctrine but to guide us in our actions to be true to the Gospel. Hear the words of St. Pope John XXIII on February 18, 1959, as he explains why private revelation happens:

> We must listen with simplicity of heart to the salutary warnings of the Mother of God. ... The Roman Pontiffs, ... if they have been constituted the guardians and interpreters of Divine Revelation contained in Scripture and Tradition, also have the duty, when after mature examination they deem it necessary for the common good of bringing to the attention of the faithful, those supernatural lights which it pleases God to dispense freely to certain privileged souls, not for the purpose of presenting new doctrines, but to guide us in our conduct.[49]

That's right. Jesus doesn't send his mother down to reveal something he forgot to say while he was on earth. In fact, the Catholic Church believes that all of what is called "Public Revelation," the saving truth of Jesus Christ transmitted to his apostles and disciples under the power of the Holy Spirit, ended with the death of St. John the Apostle.

Private revelation, on the other hand, has as its purpose to challenge us to *live* the Gospel of Jesus and the teachings of his Church — not to replace them. It's an exhortation, a call to live the most challenging aspects of the teachings of Jesus, which include things like generous prayer, fasting, penance, and ongoing conversion — things all Christians, and also, I believe, non-Christians, need to be reminded of.

Private revelation has always been part of the history of Christianity, starting in the New Testament with reports of special revelations given to certain individuals in the Acts of the Apostles.[50] In theological terms, it is part of the gift of prophecy, a gift of the Holy Spirit that informs a person of something for their own spiritual benefit or the spiritual benefit of many others as well. The term "private" in private revelation is just used to distinguish it from Public Revelation. It does not imply that the special revelation of information (if, of course, it is truly supernatural) is to be *kept* private.

Although always secondary and subordinate in importance to the Public Revelation of the Gospel, certain private revelations given to the world by Jesus or Mary have been spread globally, and rightly so — the more people know, the more they can better conform their lives to the life of Jesus, which is also his Mother's goal. (Remember her last words in Public Revelation, "Do whatever *he* tells you.")

Having served on several international commissions of investigation into private revelations, I can assure you that if it truly is Jesus or Mary, then spiritual peace rather than temporal anxiety will be the spiritual fruit of the supernatural message. This holds true even if the message accurately conveys some future elements that call for humanity's immediate attention and conversion.

Yes, whether we like it or not, we seem to be living at the climax of what has been called the "Age of Mary." This Age of Mary technically begins with the appearances of Mary known as the "Miraculous Medal Apparitions" in 1830 in Paris. This Marian Age continues into our own time with appearances and messages that beautifully and profoundly manifest the three criteria mentioned above for supernatural authenticity (for being real).

The overall Marian message to the contemporary world through these authentic Marian messages is, in essence, the same but with significant theological, historical, and cultural accents.

Here's the heart of Mary's message to our world:

- Greater faith in Jesus Christ and his Body, the Church;

- Conversion to the Gospel and away from sin;

- Fasting and penance to discipline ourselves and to offer spiritual sacrifices for others;

- The daily praying of the Rosary, which Our Lady repeatedly says has the power to change the course of human history (see Appendix One if it is new to you);

- Living in the spiritual peace of Jesus, which is precisely the spiritual fruit of greater faith, prayer, fasting, and conversion.

Still, the individual messages of the Spiritual Mother of All Peoples have a particular richness and beauty, just as Mary appears under a different face and dress in each of her apparitions. This shows Mary's motherly universality and the "beauty of diversity" found in her various apparitions.

In the final chapters that follow, I just want to whet your appetite by introducing you to a few messages from some of the major apparitions that have taken place during this Age of Mary. These brief introductions, which are just a sampling of Marian messages that make up this historic Age of Mary, will be radically insufficient to convey their sublimity and beauty. Still, I offer them with the hope that you will get to know them more deeply.

I believe these apparitions are from heaven, delivered ultimately as personal messages from our Mother to you and to me.

Chapter 12

'All Who Wear It Will
Receive Great Graces'

I want to confide to you a little rule that I had to promise myself in writing these last chapters. Why am I confiding it to you? Because they say in battling temptations, it's good to tell someone else, who can then hold you accountable. You're that someone else.

What am I confessing? My love and appreciation for our Mother's true apparitions. (From this point on, I'm often going to call her "Our Mother" or "Our Lady" out of respect for her, even though I'm not imposing that acceptance of her on you — that's your call.)

Well, what's the problem with loving her apparitions? The problem is that I am tempted to write on and on about each one, describing their full historical significance and the particular maternal love and tenderness they express. And the problem is? The problem is that's not what this short book is meant to do. It's an introduction to your Mother in general, not a whole theological treatise on her contemporary apparitions.

So, here's the commitment that you can hold me accountable to: I'll only be choosing a handful of the Marian messages granted to the world, so you can get a teaser of these motherly interventions, after which you are free (and certainly encouraged!) to pursue their full beauty. (Check out, if interested, www.motherofallpeoples.com, which offers longer articles on each of the Marian apparitions I mention here and many more.)

I also promise to keep the introduction of each Marian apparition brief, so this concise text can keep its character and purpose as a popular and short Marian handbook you can pick up, put down, or carry around with a certain ease.

I want you to sample a few of the direct messages from "our Common Mother" (to use an expression made famous by St. Pope John Paul II[51]), so you can grow accustomed to her voice, her actual words, her manner — because Our Lady's way is always a manner of motherly peace and love, even when what she says is difficult for her earthly children to hear.

One last apologetic note. To be true to the agreement of brevity, I will only be treating a few Marian messages from the modern "Age of Mary," which forces me to leave out extraordinarily beautiful messages like that of Our Lady of Guadalupe in Mexico back in 1531. The message of the "Merciful Mother" of Guadalupe comes with a scientifically documented miracle known as the "Miraculous Image" of Our Lady of Guadalupe — a supernaturally placed image of Mary on the "tilma" or poncho of the seer St. Juan Diego. It's so powerful, you don't want to miss this apparition, even though we won't deal with it directly.[52] (Did that just break the rule? I hope not.)

Okay, now, let's begin.

The modern "Age of Mary," as I mentioned before, really starts with the appearances of "Our Lady of Grace" in 1830 to St. Catherine Laboure, a religious sister in Paris. The historical climate in Paris was one of great social and political unrest, with attacks against the Church being common. (Keep in mind, this is shortly after the tragic French Revolution.)

On November 27, 1830, in the Paris convent of the Daughters of Charity, Our Lady appeared to the young sister in the following vision: Mary was standing on a globe of the earth with her foot crushing the head of a serpent. Rays of grace streamed from her outstretched hands. Around this image of Mary were the words, "O Mary, conceived without sin, pray for us who have recourse to thee."

All of a sudden, the image of Our Lady turned around, as if to show St. Catherine a second vision, one for the back of the medal she would request be struck. This second image consisted of a large "M" connected with a horizontal bar to a cross. Under the cross, two hearts were depicted: one with a crown of thorns and the other with a sword piercing it through. Around the circumference of this second vision were 12 stars.

Our Lady then gave these simple instructions: "Have a medal struck after this model. All who wear it will receive great graces. They should wear it around the neck."

Two years later, the Archbishop of Paris gave permission for the striking of this medal, which was originally called the "Medal of the Immaculate Conception." Immediately upon its distribution in Paris and beyond, the medal became the occasion for so many hundreds and even thousands of miracles that the medal was quickly nicknamed the "Miraculous Medal" by the people of the region. A formal Church investigation of the reported apparitions was soon conducted, and in 1836, the Apparitions of Our Lady of Grace were declared to be of a supernatural origin.

Very quickly (as these things go), the Miraculous Medal was spread throughout the Catholic world, leading to its direct approval by Pope Pius IX in 1842. In fact, these apparitions gave strong encouragement to Pope Pius IX to declare the dogma of the Immaculate Conception. Remember, private revelation can't be the *foundation* for a Marian dogma (that has to come from the Bible and Christian Tradition, properly interpreted by the Pope), but it can certainly act as *heaven's encouragement and confirmation* for declaring a Marian dogma.

Let's go back for a moment and appreciate the packed and powerful symbolism contained on this "miraculous" Marian medal.

We'll start with the front image. Mary is standing with her foot crushing the head of the serpent. This refers to Genesis 3:15 and the "woman" who is the mother of the seed of victory, Jesus, who will "crush the head" of Satan. That's her role as Co-redemptrix with Jesus, the Redeemer. Mary is clearly and uniquely working in union with Jesus in order to conquer Satan and sin.

Next, graces are coming forth from her outstretched hands — that's her role as the Mediatrix of all graces.

Thirdly, the prayer surrounding the image relays Our Lady's role as Advocate: "Pray for us who have recourse to thee." These inspired words ask Mary to intercede for us, as only she can.

Finally, for the front image, we have the confirmation of the doctrine of the Immaculate Conception: "O Mary, conceived without sin ...."

Now, to the back image.

The large "M" connected to a cross is yet another image of Mary as Co-redemptrix, who stands with Jesus on the Cross in their joint efforts to redeem the world. (That's the second time it has been symbolized on such a small medal. Heaven must really want us to get the Co-redemptrix role straight).

The "Two Hearts" that follow represent the suffering Hearts of Jesus and Mary. Redemption and Co-redemption once again. The theme of the "Triumph" of the Hearts of Jesus and Mary will be perhaps the strongest and most central theme throughout the entire Marian message to the modern world.

Finally, on the back, the 12 stars that encircle the image depict Mary's role as Queen in the Kingdom of God. And she who is Queen, as we discussed earlier, is also Advocate for the people to the King of God's Kingdom.

Wow — it's hard to imagine more Marian truth artistically conveyed on two sides of a one-inch medal!

This, then, is the beginning of the Age of Mary. These themes will not change but rather grow and develop, like a child in the womb, until they are more fully proclaimed and understood by the Church and the world.

Chapter 13

Our Lady of Lourdes

Mary seems to like mountains. Perhaps it's because Jerusalem is the high point of its surroundings. Perhaps it's because mountains are where God and man meet to make covenants, like with Moses and Mount Sinai. Perhaps it's where man reaches the heights of the earth and God stoops down in love to meet him there. Or perhaps it's because there's just a lot of built-in penance to get up to those pilgrimage sites!

Whatever the reason, mountains are the backdrop for the apparitions of the "Immaculate Conception" to the 14-year-old peasant girl Bernadette Soubirous amidst the stately Pyrenees in the small mountain town called Lourdes.

From February to July in 1858, Our Lady appeared some 18 times to the young French visionary. The message of Our Lady of Lourdes not only confirms the Marian dogma of the Immaculate Conception (which had been declared some four years earlier in 1854) but also conveys a message of prayer and penance to God in reparation for sin and for the conversion of sinners, the Rosary prayer, and God's desire to heal His children of illness, both spiritual and physical. Such has been the personal experience of the millions of people who have visited Lourdes since these historic apparitions.

During the sixth and eighth apparitions, the Lady instructed Bernadette: "Pray for the sinners ... . You must pray to God for sinners." Bernadette also communicated the Lady's message, "Penance, penance, penance."

There is a beautiful Christian belief that when one member of Jesus' "Mystical Body" (those people spiritually connected by the grace of Jesus) offers prayers and personal sacrifices or patiently endures suffering for another person, then *this offering has a supernatural value.* Such suffering releases graces to those in need, especially to those in need of the grace of conversion. This is similar to our previous discussion about Christians being "co-redeemers in Christ."

Such prayers and penances (for example, fastings or personal sacrifices) can also be *applied back to God himself:* to console him for the children who have rejected his love and his sacrifice on the Cross for the forgiveness of sin.

Have you ever done something really great for someone and then been disappointed to see that same person show absolutely no sign of appreciation or gratitude? Sadly, many human beings fall into this category today regarding the greatest thing ever done for any of us: Jesus' crucifixion and death.

Not only does much of humanity reject Jesus' grace and love, but they also fail to recognize the Father's gift of creation, another sin that, in the order of love, hurts the Heart of God. To love is to make oneself vulnerable, and God loves a lot.

When prayer and penance is offered by Christians directly to God to atone for the sins of others and to console the Heart of a God who loves so infinitely but has had that love rejected, it is called "reparation."

When prayer and penance is offered by Christians for the conversion of sinners, it is called "co-redemption."

The message of Lourdes calls us to both — reparation and co-redemption.

During the ninth apparition on February 25, 1858, "the Lady" instructed the young seer to uncover a miraculous spring, which is world renowned today for its spiritual and physical healings. This is Bernadette's account of the event:

> While I was in prayer, the Lady said to me in a friendly, but serious voice, "Go, drink and wash in the spring." As I did not know where this spring was, and as I did not think the matter important, I went towards the river. The Lady called me back and signed to me with her finger to go under the grotto to the left; I obeyed but I did not see any water. Not knowing where to get it from, I scratched the earth and the water came. I let it get a little clear of the mud, then I drank and washed.[53]

While there have been well over 60 documented miracles of physical healings from contact with this miraculous spring (as verified by a scrupulous international medical team there), thousands upon thousands have reported physical healings that have not gone through the medical process to verify them. Then, there are also the millions who have reported *miraculous healings of the heart* — conversions, reconciliations, the returning of love to God, faith, and family.

Jesus is the only true Healer. And he is generous, especially through the intercession of the Mediatrix of all graces, which includes the graces that lead to spiritual and physical healings.

On March 25, 1858 (feast of the Annunciation), Our Lady answered a question St. Bernadette had previously asked several times but which Mary had chosen not to answer. Here is Bernadette's account of Our Lady of Lourdes' historic self-revelation:

> "When I was on my knees before the Lady," she continued, "I asked her pardon for arriving late. Always good and gracious, she made a sign to me with her head that I need not excuse myself. Then I spoke to her of all my affection, all my respect and the happiness I had in seeing her again. After having poured out my heart to her I took up my Rosary. While I was praying, the thought of asking her name came before my mind with such persistence that I could think of nothing else. I feared to be presumptuous in repeating a question she had always refused to answer. And yet something compelled me to speak. At last, under an irresistible impulse, the words fell from my mouth, and I begged the Lady to tell me who she was. The Lady did as she had always done before; she bowed her head and smiled but she did not reply. I cannot say why, but I felt myself bolder and asked her again to graciously tell me her name; however she only bowed and smiled as before, still remaining silent. Then once more, for a third time, clasping my hands and confessing myself unworthy of the favour I was asking of her, I

again made my request ... . The Lady was standing above the rose-bush, in a position very similar to that shown in the miraculous medal. At the third request her face became very serious and she seemed to bow down in an attitude of humility. Then she joined her hands and raised them to her breast ... . She looked up to Heaven ... then slowly opening her hands and leaning forward towards me, she said to me in a voice vibrating with emotion: '*I am the Immaculate Conception*'!"

Notice Our Lady did not say "believe in the Immaculate Conception" or "I was immaculately conceived." She said, "*I am* the Immaculate Conception." As we discussed previously in the chapter on the Immaculate Conception, this is not simply another "jewel" in Mary's crown. No, as St. Maximilian Kolbe properly interpreted, it is a heavenly statement about *Mary's very being* — that she is, by God's providential blessing and the saving graces of Jesus, "full of grace" and "free from sin" in her created nature!

Penance, prayer, the Rosary — all offered in reparation to God and for the conversion of sinners.

This is the message of Our Lady of Lourdes.

Mary is the "Immaculate Conception," and she wishes to bestow the graces of holiness, healing, and sanctification on each one of us.

Chapter 14

'In the End, My Immaculate Heart Will Triumph'

The message of Fatima will really test my promise to keep things brief. So much truth, so much prophecy that has already come to pass, so much prophecy still to be fulfilled, so much relevance to today. Alright, well, I'm going to minimize my commentary and maximize your exposure to Our Lady's actual words.

Here we go.

In 1917, the Mother of Jesus appeared to three Portuguese children: Lucia (age 10), Francisco (age 8), and Jacinta (age 7), in the country village of Fatima. Her title at Fatima is "Our Lady of the Rosary," and her message (as a further development of the Lourdes message but with more specific directions) can be summarized as follows:

1. Prayer, daily Rosary, and penance to God in reparation for sins and for the conversion of sinners. (Sound familiar?)
2. A special "First Saturday devotion" that is to be offered in specific reparation to the "Immaculate Heart of Mary."

3. Prophecies of *conditional* upcoming challenges for the world if the world would not convert. (Remember, these were given in 1917.) These challenges include the following: a second world war, the rise of widespread Communism, the annihilation of various nations, persecutions of the Church and specifically of the Holy Father, and a "third secret" concerning future Church and world affairs.

4. The remedy for these challenges in the form of a "consecration" (or special entrusting) of Russia to the Immaculate Heart by the Pope and the ongoing offering of the "First Saturday" devotion of Reparation to Mary's Immaculate Heart.

Pow! That's a mouthful. I know there are a lot of individual themes here, but a few of Our Lady's actual messages from Fatima will explain a lot.

We'll start with what many people think is the single most important Marian message of the 20th century. Mary revealed it to the children on July 13, 1917, and the following account is from the memoirs of the principal Fatima seer, Lucia. It's long but certainly worth the read:

A few moments after arriving at the Cova da Iria, near the holmoak, where a large number of people were praying the Rosary, we saw the flash of light once more, and a moment later Our Lady appeared on the holmoak.

"What do you want of me?" I [Lucia] asked.

"I want you to come here on the 13th of the next month, to continue to pray the Rosary every day in honor of Our Lady of the Rosary, in order to obtain peace for the world and the end of the war, because only she can help you … ."

"Sacrifice yourselves for sinners, and say many times, especially whenever you make some sacrifice: O Jesus, it is for love of You, for the conversion of sinners, and in reparation for the sins committed against the Immaculate Heart of Mary."

As Our Lady spoke these last words, she opened her hands once more, as she had done during the two previous months. The rays of light seemed to penetrate the earth, and we saw, as it were, a sea of fire. Plunged in this fire were demons and souls in human form, like transparent burning embers, all blackened or burnished bronze, floating about in the conflagration, now raised into the air by the flames that issued from within themselves together with great clouds of smoke, now falling back on every side like sparks in huge fires, without weight or equilibrium, amid shrieks and groans of pain and despair, which horrified us and made us tremble with fear. (It must have been this sight which caused me to cry out, as people say they heard me.) The demons could be distinguished by their terrifying and repellent likeness to frightful and unknown animals, black and transparent like burning coals. Terrified and as if to plead for succor, we looked up to Our Lady, who said to us, so kindly and sadly:

"You have seen hell where the souls of poor sinners go. To save them, God wishes to establish in the world devotion to my Immaculate Heart. If what I say to you is done, many souls will be saved and there will be peace. The war is going to end; but if people do not cease offending God, a worse one will break out during the pontificate of Pius XI. When you see a night illuminated by an unknown light, know that this is the great sign given you by God that he is about to punish the world for its crimes, by means of war, famine, and persecutions of the Church and the Holy Father.

"To prevent this, I shall come to ask for the consecration of Russia to my Immaculate Heart, and the Communion of Reparation on the First Saturdays. If my requests are heeded, Russia will be converted, and there will be peace; if not, she will spread her errors throughout the world, causing wars and persecutions of the Church. The good will be martyred, the Holy Father will have much to suffer, various nations will be annihilated. In the end, my Immaculate Heart will triumph. The Holy Father will consecrate Russia to me, and she will be converted, and a period of peace will be granted to the world. In Portugal, the dogma of the Faith will always be preserved … .

"When you pray the Rosary, say after each mystery: O my Jesus, forgive us our sins, save us from the fires of hell. Lead all souls to Heaven, especially those who are most in need of Thy mercy."[54]

Let me offer just a few thoughts about this monumental Fatima message.

The call to pray the Rosary daily in order to "obtain peace for the world" is clear enough. The message is given during World War I, and it specifies "only she can help you." That's because the task of bringing peace to the world has been given by God to Mary. This returns us to her role as the Mediatrix of all graces, which includes the graces necessary for world peace.

The vision of hell is to remind the world that "hell is real." But notice that Our Lady of Fatima offers a remedy, which is precisely *devotion and consecration to her Immaculate Heart.* (See Appendix Two to learn more about Marian consecration.) Her Immaculate Heart is a symbol of her pure, perfect love for humanity, which is a motherly reflection of the love of Jesus' "Sacred Heart" for us.

Some of the Fatima messages predicted punishments for the world that have already happened: for example, World War II and the spread of Communism coming from Russia.

Our Lady's request to "consecrate Russia to her Immaculate Heart" was satisfied when, on March 25, 1984, St. Pope John Paul II consecrated the world, inclusive of Russia, to her Immaculate Heart. Still, her requests for prayers must continue to be answered as the tragic effects of atheistic Communism remain with us today.

Mary's promise of victory comes "at the end": "In the end, My Immaculate Heart will triumph ... and a period of peace will be granted to the world." Many believe that for this "Triumph" of Mary's Heart to be complete, we need the proclamation of Mary, Co-Redemptrix, Mediatrix, and Advocate as a dogma. This is so that, by our free consent, she can be "released" to intercede to her maximum capacity to bring peace to the world. (A quick examination of the world scene makes clear that Mary's "Triumph" and its effect of world peace have not yet been realized on a global level.)

Now, having looked at what many call the most important Fatima message, let's turn our attention to some of the other most famous and important messages.

On October 13, 1917, a great "Solar Miracle" took place, which was witnessed by more than *70,000 onlookers.* They described the sun as "dancing in the sky," giving off various colors, spinning like a disc, and then appearing to approach the earth, only later to return to its position in the sky. Here's Our Lady's October 13, 1917, Fatima message:

"I want to tell you that a chapel is to be built here in my honour. I am the Lady of the Rosary. Continue always to pray the Rosary every day. The war is going to end, and the soldiers will soon return to their homes."

Lucia: "I have many things to ask you: the cure of some sick persons, the conversion of sinners and other things … ."

"Some yes, but not others. They must amend their lives and ask for forgiveness for their sins."

Looking very sad, Our Lady said:

"Do not offend the Lord our God anymore, because he is already so much offended."

Then, opening her hands, she made them reflect on the sun, and as she ascended, the reflection of her own light continued to be projected on the sun itself. …

After Our Lady had disappeared into the immense distance of the firmament, we beheld St. Joseph with the Child Jesus and Our Lady robed in white with a blue mantle, beside the sun. St. Joseph and the Child Jesus appeared to bless the world, for they traced the Sign of the Cross with their hands. When, a little later, this apparition disappeared, I saw Our Lord and Our Lady; it seemed to me that it was Our Lady of Dolours. Our Lord appeared to bless the world in the same manner as St. Joseph had done. This apparition also vanished, and I saw Our Lady once more, this time resembling Our Lady of Carmel.

Notice how Mary appears first with the Holy Family. (Also notice that St. Joseph, as "Patron of the Church," blessed the world along with the Infant Jesus). Next, Mary appears as the "Co-Redemptrix" or Our Lady of Sorrows. Thirdly, she appears as Our Lady of Mt. Carmel with a scapular in her hand.

These three visions represent the three sets of mysteries of the Rosary up to that point in history: the Joyful Mysteries, focusing on the birth of Jesus; the Sorrowful Mysteries, which focus on Jesus' Passion and Mary's co-suffering; and the Glorious Mysteries, focusing on eternal life.

A "seventh" key message of Fatima took place on December 10, 1925. The little visionary, Lucia, later became Sr. Lucia, and Mary appeared to her with an extremely important message about the "First Saturday Devotion of Reparation." Here's the message from Sr. Lucia's memoirs: (By the way, Sr. Lucia refers to herself as "her" in the third person, as was the custom in her day.)

On December 10, 1925, the most holy Virgin appeared to her, and by her side, elevated by a luminous cloud, was a child. The most holy Virgin rested her hand on her shoulder, and as she did so, she showed her a heart encircled by thorns, which she was holding in her hand. At the same time, the Child said:

"Have compassion on the Heart of your most holy Mother, covered with thorns, with which ungrateful men pierce it at every moment, and there is no one to make an act of reparation to remove them."

Then, the most holy Virgin said:

"Look, my daughter, at my Heart, surrounded with thorns with which ungrateful men pierce me at every moment by their blasphemies and ingratitude. You at least try to console me, and say that I promise to assist at the hour of death, with the graces necessary for salvation, all those who, on the first Saturday of five consecutive months, shall confess, receive Holy Communion, recite five decades of the Rosary, and keep me company for fifteen minutes while meditating on the fifteen mysteries of the Rosary, with the intention of making reparation to me."

See how both Jesus and Our Lady speak about the ongoing sufferings of Mary's Immaculate Heart? Of course, this makes sense. If you saw every sin committed by the human family today and you had the unique role of being the Spiritual Mother of all humanity, your heart would be suffering as well. That's why the intention for performing and offering these Five First Saturday devotions must be made *specifically in reparation to Mary's Immaculate Heart.*

So, the four specific acts to perform for five First Saturdays (and perpetually, for those who understand how much Mary's Heart continues to suffer) are as follows:

1. Receive the Sacrament of Confession or Reconciliation (within two weeks of the First Saturday);
2. Receive Holy Communion;
3. Pray five decades of the Rosary;
4. Meditate for 15 minutes on any of the mysteries of the Rosary.

In June of 2000, St. Pope John Paul II chose to publicly release what is known as the "Third Secret of Fatima." Recall the first Fatima message we looked at, which was revealed on July 13, 1917. A the end of that message, Our Lady revealed a third part (after the first part, the vision of hell and the second part, the devotion to the Immaculate Heart), which, Mary said to the young Lucia, had to remain secret until a later time.

Well, St. Pope John Paul II (who Sr. Lucia said was the "Bishop dressed in white" found in the Secret), decided that it was the right time. Here are the contents of the Third Secret, which he disclosed to the world:

After the two parts which I have already explained, at the left of Our Lady and a little above, we saw an Angel with a flaming sword in his left hand; flashing, it gave out flames that looked as though they would set the world on fire; but they died out in contact with the splendour that Our Lady radiated towards him from her right hand: pointing to the earth with his right hand, the Angel cried out in a loud voice: "Penance, Penance, Penance!" And we saw in an immense light that is God: "something similar to how people appear in a mirror when they pass in front of it" a Bishop dressed in White "we had the impression that it was the Holy Father" and other Bishops, Priests, men and women Religious going up a steep mountain, at the top of which there was a big Cross of rough-hewn trunks as of a cork-tree with the bark; before reaching there the Holy Father passed through a big city half in ruins and half trembling with halting step, afflicted with pain and sorrow, he prayed for the souls of the corpses he met on his way; having reached the top of the mountain, on his knees at the foot of the big Cross he was killed by a group of soldiers who fired bullets and arrows at him, and in the same way there died one after another the other Bishops, Priests, men and women Religious, and various lay people of different ranks and positions. Beneath the two arms of the Cross there were two Angels each with a crystal aspersorium in his hand, in which they gathered up the blood of the Martyrs and with it sprinkled the souls that were making their way to God.

Now, there is no official interpretation of the Third Secret by the Church, but Cardinal Joseph Ratzinger (who history now knows as Pope Emeritus Benedict XVI) said that modern humanity has the capacity to carry out the kind of destruction mentioned in Fatima. (Think of our frightful nuclear capacity.) In view of this, Pope Benedict underscored the great relevance of the Fatima message for today.

Regarding one thing, we can rest assured — Our Lady keeps her promises. If she promised that "in the end, My Immaculate Heart will triumph," then it will. I recommend we each do our own small part of Rosary, devotion, and reparation to the Immaculate Heart, and offer it toward the fulfillment of this Triumph — for the historic fruit of a worldwide "era of peace."

Conclusion

Drawing Closer to a Mother's Love

I hope that in some small way, this short introduction on Mary has helped you consider opening your heart and accepting the woman, the Mother, Jesus gave you from the Cross. I also hope it has left you with a desire to grow even closer to her. If so, then there are two things that I highly recommend that you do.

First, pray the Rosary every day. (See Appendix One on how to pray it.) The Rosary is a beautiful combination of vocal prayer and meditation that centers on the greatest Gospel mysteries in the life of Jesus Christ and secondarily in the life of the Lord's mother. It's a way of staying in touch with your Mother. It's also a way of going "to Jesus through Mary," which, according to the saints, is the best way to grow in holiness! Which brings me to my second recommendation: Marian Consecration (also known as "Marian entrustment").

According to St. Louis de Montfort, total consecration to Jesus through Mary is the "quickest, easiest, surest way" to grow in holiness. It's the best way I know of to draw closer to our Mother's love and to accept the gift of Mary in our lives. In Appendix Two, I've included a brief excerpt from the introduction of *33 Days to Morning Glory*, an excellent consecration manual which explains the meaning of Marian consecration.

Whether or not you pray the Rosary every day or decide to consecrate yourself to Jesus through Mary — I hope you do! — please know that your Heavenly Mother will continue to intercede for you and do everything in her power to unite you more intimately to Jesus, and she will always love you unconditionally with a mother's heart.

That's what mothers do. That's what Mary does for you — now and for all time.

Now, as we draw things to a close, I'd like to leave you with a final word to ponder in your heart: Now that you know your Mother more, please don't be afraid to fall in love with her! In other words, don't be afraid to love her "too much." Why should we not be afraid? Let me explain.

Our love for Mary will never equal the love that Jesus has for her. And while it's true that some people could have some type of disordered, even fanatical attachment to Mary (one that is not based on the Christian truth about her, but rather on some religious error or psychological abnormality), this actually would not be "too much love" but rather "too little love," based on a mistake.

In short, you cannot love Mary too much because your love for her will never match Jesus' love for her. Also, a true love for Mary actually leads to a greater love for Jesus, not to the terrible mistake of making Mary into a "goddess."

I think Blessed Mother Teresa best summarizes for us why we should love Mary and hold her in the greatest esteem. Once, when she was seated on a plane, a friendly admirer said, "Mother, I greatly respect all you do for the poor and your witness to charity. But I just can't understand your devotion to Mary." Mother Teresa looked at her with a smile and responded, "My dear, it is simple: *No Mary, no Jesus.*"

Appendices

Appendix 1

How To Pray the Rosary

The Rosary begins by holding the Crucifix and making the Sign of the Cross as we pray:

The Sign of the Cross

In the name of the Father, and of the Son, and of the Holy Spirit. Amen.

While still holding the Crucifix, we profess our beliefs as we pray:

The Apostles' Creed

I believe in God, the Father almighty, Creator of heaven and earth, and in Jesus Christ, his only Son, our Lord, who was conceived by the Holy Spirit, born of the Virgin Mary, suffered under Pontius Pilate, was crucified, died and was buried; he descended into hell; on the third day he rose again from the dead; he ascended into heaven, and is seated at the right hand of God the Father almighty; from there he will come to judge the living and the dead. I believe in the Holy Spirit, the holy catholic Church, the communion of saints, the forgiveness of sins, the resurrection of the body, and life everlasting. Amen.

On the first bead, we pray the Our Father. This is traditionally offered for the intention of the Holy Father, the Pope:

Our Father

Our Father, who art in heaven, hallowed be thy name; thy kingdom come; thy will be done on earth as it is in heaven. Give us this day our daily bread; and forgive us our trespasses, as we forgive those who trespass against us; and lead us not into temptation, but deliver us from evil. Amen.

Three Hail Marys are then prayed for the virtues of faith, hope, and charity:

Hail Mary

Hail, Mary, full of grace; the Lord is with thee; blessed art thou among women, and blessed is the fruit of thy womb, Jesus. Holy Mary, Mother of God, pray for us sinners, now and at the hour of our death. Amen.

We then pray the Glory Be (no bead):

Glory Be

Glory be to the Father, and to the Son, and to the Holy Spirit. As it was in the beginning is now, and ever shall be, world without end. Amen.

On the fifth bead, we announce* the first mystery (see list of mysteries below) and while meditating on the mystery say one Our Father and ten Hail Marys (one on each of the next ten beads) and a Glory Be (no bead.) Then, as requested by Our Lady of the Rosary at Fatima, we pray:

Fatima Prayer

O my Jesus, forgive us our sins, save us from the fires of Hell. Lead all souls to Heaven, especially those who are most in need of Thy mercy.

(Repeat from * for each mystery.)

At the end of the five decades, the "Hail, Holy Queen" is prayed:

Hail, Holy Queen

Hail! Holy Queen, Mother of Mercy, our life, our sweetness, and our hope. To thee do we cry, poor banished children of Eve; to thee do we send up our sighs, mourning and weeping in this valley of tears. Turn then, most gracious Advocate, thine eyes of mercy toward us; and after this our exile show unto us the blessed fruit of thy womb, Jesus. O clement, O loving, O sweet Virgin Mary.

V. Pray for us, O holy Mother of God.

R. That we may be made worthy of the promises of Christ.

Optional Closing Prayer from the Roman Missal:

O God, whose only-begotten Son, by his life, death, and resurrection, has purchased for us the rewards of eternal life; grant, we beseech you, that, while meditating on these mysteries of the most holy Rosary of the Blessed Virgin Mary, we may imitate what they contain, and obtain what they promise. Through the same Christ our Lord. Amen.

End with the Sign of the Cross.

The Twenty Mysteries of the Rosary

Joyful Mysteries

1. *The Annunciation* — "Hail, full of grace, the Lord is with thee. Blessed art thou among women" (Lk 1:28).
2. *The Visitation* — "When Elizabeth heard the greeting of Mary the babe in her womb leapt, and she was filled with the Holy Spirit" (Lk 1:41).
3. *The Birth of Jesus* — "And she brought forth her firstborn Son and wrapped Him in swaddling clothes" (Lk 2:7).
4. *The Presentation* — "According to the law of Moses, they took Jesus up to Jerusalem to present Him to the Lord" (Lk 2:32).
5. *The Finding of the Child Jesus in the Temple* — "After three days they found Him in the temple. He was sitting in the midst of the teachers" (Lk 2:45, 46).

Luminous Mysteries

6. *The Baptism of the Lord* — "This is My beloved Son, with whom I am well pleased" (Mt 3:17).
7. *The Wedding at Cana* — "His mother said to the servants, 'Do whatever He tells you'" (Jn 2:5).
8. *The Proclamation of the Kingdom of God* — "The kingdom of God is at hand; repent, and believe in the gospel" (Mk 1:15).
9. *The Transfiguration* — "As He was praying, the appearance of His countenance was altered, and His raiment became dazzling white. And behold, two men talked with Him, Moses and Elijah, who appeared in

glory and spoke of His departure, which He was to accomplish at Jerusalem" (Lk 9: 29-31).

10. *The Institution of the Eucharist* — "And He took bread, and when He had given thanks He broke it and gave it to them, saying, 'This is My body which is given for you. Do this in remembrance of Me'" (Lk 22:19).

Sorrowful Mysteries

11. *The Agony in the Garden* — "Jesus came with them to Gethsemane and He began to be saddened and exceedingly troubled" (Mt 26:36, 37).
12. *The Scourging at the Pillar* — "Pilate then took Jesus and had Him scourged" (Jn 19:1).
13. *The Crowning of Thorns* — "And plaiting a crown of thorns they put it upon His Head and a reed into His right hand" (Mt 27:29)
14. *Jesus Carries the Cross* — "And bearing the Cross for Himself, He went forth to the place called The Skull" (Jn 19:1).
15. *The Crucifixion* — "And when they came to the place called The Skull they crucified Him" (Lk 23:33).

Glorious Mysteries

16. *The Resurrection* — "He is not here, but has risen. Behold the place where they laid Him" (Lk 24:6; Mk 16:19).
17. *The Ascension* — "And He was taken up into Heaven and sits at the right hand of God" (Mk 16:19).
18. *The Descent of the Holy Spirit* — "And suddenly there came a sound from Heaven ... and there appeared to

them parted tongues of fire ... and they were filled with the Holy Spirit" (Acts 2:2, 3, 4, 11).

19. *The Assumption of Mary, Body and Soul into Heaven* — "Hear, O daughter, and see; turn your ear, for the King shall desire your beauty. All glorious is the king's daughter as she enters: her raiment is threaded with spun gold" (Ps 44:11, 12, 14).

20. *The Coronation of Mary, Queen of Heaven and Earth* — "And a great sign appeared in Heaven: a woman clothed with the sun, and the moon under her feet, and upon her head a crown of twelve stars" (Rev 12:1).

Note: If five decades are prayed daily, the general order suggested by St. Pope John Paul II in his apostolic letter on the Rosary, *Rosarium Virginis Mariae* (no. 38), is that the Joyful Mysteries are prayed on Monday and Saturday, the Luminous Mysteries on Thursday, the Sorrowful Mysteries on Tuesday and Friday, and the Glorious Mysteries on Wednesday and Sunday. However, during the Advent and Christmas seasons, the Joyful Mysteries are often prayed on Sundays. Likewise, during the season of Lent, the Sorrowful Mysteries are often prayed on Sundays.

Appendix 2

Introduction to Marian Consecration

[This appendix is as an excerpt from the Marian Press title *33 Days to Morning Glory: A Do-It-Yourself Retreat in Preparation for Marian Consecration* by Fr. Michael Gaitley, MIC.]

Marian consecration is all about a new way of life in Christ. The act of consecrating oneself to Jesus through Mary marks the beginning of a gloriously new day, a new dawn, a brand new morning in one's spiritual journey. It's a fresh start, and it changes everything.

As St. Louis de Montfort noted in his book *True Devotion to Mary*, Marian consecration is a "short, easy, secure, and perfect" way to become a saint. Saint John Paul II even says that reading de Montfort's book was a "turning point in his life."[55] In fact, his consecration to Jesus through Mary was so important to him that he adopted as his papal motto de Montfort's own words that summarize total consecration to Jesus through Mary, "*Totus Tuus*" ("Totally Yours"). Also, it's reported that the Pope recited the long version of de Montfort's consecration prayer every day.

Many who have consecrated themselves to Jesus through Mary completely relate to the Pope's words about how it's a turning point in one's life — or a gloriously new morning in one's spiritual journey. It truly does make a difference. It truly is "the surest, easiest, shortest, and the most perfect means" to become a saint.

What is Marian Consecration?

To properly understand the essence of total consecration to Jesus through Mary, we'll first need to reflect on an important point: Jesus wants to include all of us in his work of salvation. In other words, he doesn't just redeem us and then expect us to kick back and relax. On the contrary, he puts us to work. He wants all of us to labor in his Father's vineyard in one way or another. Why he didn't just snap his fingers and so order things that everyone in the world would individually hear and understand the Gospel by some private, mystical revelation, we don't know. What we do know is that Jesus relies on others to spread his Gospel and that he commissions his disciples to preach it to all (see Mt 28:19-20). He basically says to them and to us, "Let's get to work!" Of course, that God wants to include us in his work of salvation is a great gift and glorious privilege. Truly, there's no more important work to be done.

While everyone is called to lend a hand in the great work of salvation, not everyone has the same role. For example, St. Paul says, "There are varieties of service and ... there are varieties of working" (1 Cor 12:5-6). He goes on to say that God has appointed to the work of salvation "first apostles, second prophets, third teachers, then workers of miracles, then healers, helpers, administrators" (v. 28). Whoever we are, God has appointed us to a special task in his great work.

Among the various roles God has given to his children, there's one that's radically more important than all the others: the task he gave to Mary. We all know that God uniquely blessed Mary by choosing her to conceive, bear, and nurture Jesus Christ, our Savior. But do we also realize that her blessed work didn't end once Jesus left home and began his public ministry? After the three years of Mary's hidden life during Jesus' public ministry, Jesus brought her back into the picture of his work of salvation at its most crucial time, the "hour" of his Passion. At that hour, we might say he fully revealed Mary's special task — the same task she had begun some 33 years before and that she still continues.

Jesus fully revealed Mary's special task shortly before his death. It happened when he looked down from the Cross and said to Mary as she stood with the Apostle John, "Woman, behold, your son" and to John, "Behold, your mother" (Jn 19:26-27). At that moment, Jesus gave us one of his greatest gifts: his mother as our mother. Of course, Mary isn't our natural mother. She's our spiritual mother. In other words, just as it was once her task some 2,000 years ago to give birth to Christ, to feed and nurture him, and to help him grow and develop into a man, so also, from the time she first said yes to being the mother of Jesus until the end of time, Mary's task is to give spiritual birth to Christians, to feed and nurture them with grace, and to help them grow to full stature in Christ. In short, Mary's job is to help us grow in holiness. It's her mission to form us into saints.

"Now, wait just a minute," someone might say, "isn't it the job of the Holy Spirit to make us holy?" Indeed, it is. The Holy Spirit is the Sanctifier. It is he who transforms us at our Baptism from being mere creatures into members of the Body of Christ, and it is he who helps us in our ongoing transformation into Christ through continued conversion. Great. So how does Mary come into all of this?

Mary is the spouse of the Holy Spirit. At the Annunciation, the angel Gabriel declared to Mary that she would conceive and bear a Son and that the Holy Spirit would overshadow her (see Lk 1:31-35). When Mary said, "Behold, I am the handmaid of the Lord; let it be to me according to your word" (Lk 1:38), we can see most clearly that she's the spouse of the Holy Spirit, for at that moment, she gave the Holy Spirit permission to conceive Christ in her womb. Thus, at that moment, the already unfathomably deep bond between Mary and the Holy Spirit that had begun (in time) at the first moment of her Immaculate Conception was revealed as nothing less than a two-become-one marital union (see Gen 2:24). As a result of that union, the Holy Spirit is pleased to work and act through his spouse, Mary, for the sanctification of the human race. Of course, he didn't have to be so united to Mary. It was his free choice (and that of the Father and the Son), and in that choice he takes delight.

So, it's Mary's great God-given task, in union with and by the power of the Holy Spirit, to form every human being into "another Christ," that is, to unite everyone to the Body of Christ and form each person into a fully mature member of this Body.[56] Therefore, every human being is invited to rest in the womb of Mary and be transformed there, by the power of the Holy Spirit, more perfectly into Christ's own image. Yes, if we want to become more fully Christ, then we need to belong more fully to Mary. By going to her and remaining with her, we allow her to accomplish her mission in us. We allow her to form us into other Christs, into great saints. But how do we do this? How do we belong more fully to Mary and allow her to fulfill her mission in us? Simple. We say yes, just like she did.

Mary has a deep respect for human freedom. She knows from her own experience in Nazareth what a free yes to God can do (see Lk 1:38), and so she doesn't pressure us into giving her our yes. Of course, she always cares for her children, but she won't force us to enter into a deeper relationship with her. She surely invites us to such a relationship and patiently waits for us to accept her invitation, but she remains respectful. Still, if we could see how much longing hides behind her silence, we'd say yes to her if only to give her relief. In fact, saying yes to her gives her more than relief. It gives her joy. Great joy. And the more fully we say yes to Mary, the more joyful she becomes. For our yes gives her the freedom to complete her work in us, the freedom to form us into great saints. This brings us to the essence of what Marian consecration is all about.

Marian consecration basically means giving Mary our full permission (or as much permission as we can) to complete her motherly task in us, which is to form us into other Christs. Thus, by consecrating ourselves to Mary, each of us is saying to her:

> Mary, I want to be a saint. I know that you also want me to be a saint and that it's your God-given mission to form me into one. So, Mary, at this moment, on this day, I freely choose to give you my

full permission to do your work in me, with your Spouse, the Holy Spirit.

As soon as Mary hears us make such a decision, she flies to us and begins working a masterpiece of grace within our souls. She continues this work for as long as we don't deliberately choose to change our choice from a yes to a no, as long as we don't take back our permission and leave her. That being said, it's always a good idea for us to strive to deepen our "yes" to Mary. For the deeper our "yes" becomes, the more marvelously she can perform her works of grace in our souls.

One of the aspects of being consecrated to Mary is that she's such a gentle mother. She makes the lessons of the Cross into something sweet, and she pours her motherly love and solace into our every wound. What joy it is to be consecrated to Jesus through Mary!

To learn more about how you can get started with your own preparation for total consecration to Jesus through Mary, please see the information on the pages that follow or simply visit MarianConsecration.com.

Endnotes

Endnotes

Chapter 1

[1] Christmas Day Homily, 1529, cf. *Luther's Works* (Weimar), 10:71:19-73:2); 11:224:8, 29:655:26-656:7; as quoted in F. Mateo, *Refuting the Attacks on Mary* (Catholic Answers, 1999), p. 39.

Chapter 2

[2] Martin Luther, Commentary on the Magnificat; cf. *Luther's Works*, 22:492-94; Pelikan, ed, *Luther's Works*, 24:107.

Chapter 3

[3] Saint Pope Leo, *Tome to Flavian*, 449.

[4] Second Vatican Council, *Lumen Gentium*, n. 57; *Catechism of the Catholic Church*, n. 449.

[5] Cf. As quoted in Augustine Bea, "Mary and the Protestants," *Marian Studies*, 83, April, 1961, 1.

[6] See, for example, Mt 12:46; Mk 3:31.

[7] See, for example, Gen 13:8; Gen 29:15.

[8] *Luther's Works*, Vol. 22, 23, as quoted in "Refuting the Attacks on Mary," p. 16.

[9] As quoted in Bernard Leeming, "Protestants and Our Lady," *Marian Studies*, 128/129, Jan. 1967, p. 17.

Chapter 4

[10] Blessed Pope Pius IX, *Ineffabilis Deus*, Dec. 8, 1854.

[11] See. St. Ephraem, *Sermones exegetici, opera Omnia syriace et latine*, 2, Rome, 1740, 327.

[12] Saint Ambrose, *Exposito in Psalm 118,* Sermon 22, n. 30, PL 15, 1599.

[13] Severus, *Hom., Cathedralis, 67, PO*, 8, 350.

[14] Theognostes, *Hom. in Dorm. Deiparae*, PO, Graffin-Nau, 16, 467.

[15] Note: The Genesis 3:15 translation used in papal texts from the mid-nineteenth century up until the 1980s, where the pronoun is "she" rather than "he." Theologically, the pronoun gender does not determine the fact that, regardless of whether the pronoun is "she" or "he," the context of the passage makes clear that the woman intimately participates with her "seed of victory" — that is, Jesus Christ in his victory over Satan. The prophetic fulfillment of the passage refers to Mary, who crushes Satan's head by the power of Jesus (cf. also Rev 12 as the other "bookend" of the Bible which reveals the great battle between Mary, God's greatest creature, and Satan, God's most evil creature).

[16] See Blessed Duns Scotus, *Perservative Redemption*, for example, Miravalle, *Introduction to Mary*, Queenship Publications, p. 71.

[17] *Luther's Works*, Vol. 43, p. 40.

[18] Michael E. Gaitley, MIC, *33 Days to Morning Glory* (Stockbridge, Mass.: Marian Press, 2011), p. 52.

[19] H. M. Manteau-Bonamy, OP, *Immaculate Conception and the Holy Spirit*, trans. Richard Arnandez, FSC (Libertyville, Ill.: Franciscan Marytown Press, 1977), pp. 4-5.

[20] Ibid.

Chapter 5

[21] Venerable Pope Pius XII, *Munificentissimus Deus*, Nov. 1, 1950.

[22] Cf. Rom 5-8; Heb 2.

[23] See *Catechism of the Catholic Church*, n. 988.

[24] Saint Pope John Paul II, General Audience of June 25, 1997, *L'Osservatore Romano*, English Edition, July 7, 1997, p. 11.

[25] See, for example, 1 Cor 15:18.

Chapter 6

[26] For example, M. Miravalle, *Introduction to Mary*, Chapter 6; "With Jesus: The Story of Mary Co-redemptrix," Chapter 4; "Mary Co-redemptrix, Mediatrix, Advocate," Chs 1-2.

[27] Vatican II, *Lumen Gentium*, 61.

Chapter 7

[28] Saint Pope John Paul II, "Address to the Sick," January 13, 1982.

[29] Pope Benedict XVI, "Address to the Sick at Fatima," May 13, 2011.

[30] See, for example, references to the "Suffering Servant" in Is 53:3-5.

[31] Saint Pope John Paul II, "Homily at Marian Shrine in Guayaquil," Ecuador, Jan. 31, 1985.

[32] See, for example, Pope Leo XIII, *Jucunda Semper*, 1894.

[33] Pope Benedict XV, *Inter Sodalicia*, 1918, AAS, 10, p. 182.

[34] Saint Justin Martyr, *Dialogue with Trypho*, C. 100, PG 6, p. 719.

[35] Vatican II, *Lumen Gentium*, 58.

[36] Saint Pope John Paul II, "Homily at Our Lady of Alborada Shrine, Guayaquil, Ecuador," Jan. 31, 1985.

Chapter 8

[37] Saint Pope John Paul II, "Mary Mediatrix," Wednesday Audience Address, October 1, 1997.

[38] Pope Benedict XVI, *Latin Letter of Jan. 21 Regarding Papal Representative for the 2013 World Day of Sick*, released February 11, 2013.

[39] For example, see Antipater of Bostra, *In S. Joannem Bapt.*, PG 85, 1772 c. St. Cyril of Alexandria, Homily at Council of Ephesus, PG 65, p. 681.

Chapter 10

[40] See Canon 212, 1983 *Code of Canon Law.*

[41] See *Vox Populi Mariae Mediatrici* statistics as found on www.fifthmariandogma.com.

[42] See Fr. Peter Damien Fehlner, *Testimony of History of the Immaculate Conception,* Our Lady of Guadalupe Shrine, La Cross, Wisconsin, U.S.A, October, 2012.

[43] Bishop Josef Maria Punt, *Declaration of Supernatural Authenticity Regarding the Amsterdam Aparitions,* May 31, 2002, Diocese of Haarlem-Amsterdam Website.

[44] See Dr. Richard Russell, "The Messages of the Lady of All Nations and Why We Should Listen," *Mother of All Peoples,* Ezine; also *Peace Through A Woman* documentary, Global Outlook Productions, May 2012.

[45] May 31, 1954, Message of the Lady of All Nations.

[46] The original phrase "who once was Mary" was changed to "the Blessed Virgin Mary" in 2006 at the request of the Vatican's Congregation for the Doctrine on Faith so as to avoid any pastoral misunderstanding.

[47] Thirty-eighth Apparition, December 31, 1951.

[48] Forty-sixth Apparition, May 10, 1953.

Chapter 11

[49] Saint Pope John XXIII, "Closing Statement of the Marian Year," February 18, 1959.

[50] See, for example, Agabus and the four daughters, Acts 21:9-10.

Chapter 12

[51] See St. Pope John Paul II, encyclical *Redemptoris Mater,* 1987, n. 34.

[52] For more information on Our Lady of Guadalupe and her appearances to St. Juan Diego, please visit the Marians' link to EWTN and its resources at marianweb.net/guadalupe.

Chapter 13

[53] This quote and all other quotes of St. Bernadette Soubirous and accounts of Lourdes taken from J.B. Estrade, J.H. Girolestone, tr., *The Appearance of the Blessed Virgin Mary at the Grotto of Lourdes*, (Westminster: Art and Book Co., Ltd., 1912).

Chapter 14

[54] This quote and all other quotes from Lucia and the account of Fatima taken from *Fatima in Lucia's Own Words: Sister Lucia's Memoirs*, ed. Kondar, SVD, Postulation Center, distributed by Our Blessed Lady of Victory Mission, Brookings, South Dakota, 1976.

Appendix 2

[55] Address to the de Montfort Fathers, cited in *True Devotion*, p. vi.

[56] Mary's specially appointed task in the work of salvation does not in any way detract from Christ as the one who perfectly completes this work in himself. That Christ shares this work with Mary (and all of us) shows forth its greatness. Thus, the *Catechism* (citing the Second Vatican Council document, *Lumen Gentium* 60, 62) states:

> Mary's function as mother of men in no way obscures or diminishes [the] unique mediation of Christ, but rather shows its power. But the Blessed Virgin's salutary influence on men ... flows forth from the superabundance of the merits of Christ, rests on his mediation, depends entirely on it, and draws all its power from it.
>
> ... No creature could ever be counted along with the Incarnate Word and Redeemer; but just as the priesthood of Christ is shared in various ways both by his ministers and the faithful, and as the one goodness of God is radiated in different ways among his creatures, so also the unique mediation of the Redeemer does not exclude but rather gives rise to a manifold cooperation which is but a sharing in this one source (**970**).

Here's How the Group Retreat Works:

1. Gather a group.
Better yet, gather several groups of six to twelve people who want to consecrate themselves to Jesus through Mary.

2. Find a place to meet.
Ideally, this would be at a parish with the permission of the pastor, but your group can also meet at someone's home.

3. Read, Ponder, Meet ("RPM")
Get revved up! and...

- *Read...*
  Read the daily meditation in the retreat book, *33 Days to Morning Glory.*

- *Ponder...*
  Ponder the daily meditation with the help of the *Retreat Companion.*

- *Meet...*
  Meet with your group for weekly prayer, discussion, and to watch the accompanying talks on DVD.

Here's What You'll Need:

(Details to follow.)

1. The Retreat Book

Everyone will need
one of these.

2. The *Retreat Companion*

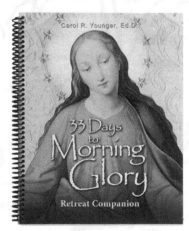

Everyone will need one
of these, too.

3. DVD Set

Just the Retreat Coordinator will need this.

How to Get What You'll Need:

1. Choose a Retreat Coordinator

The Retreat Coordinator is the person who will organize and run the group retreat.

(The responsibilities of the Retreat Coordinator are explained in the video tutorial and free, downloadable guide available at our website, AllHeartsAfire.org.)

2. Order Your Retreat Materials

Typically, the Retreat Coordinator orders all the materials for the group retreat at the same time to save on shipping. But anyone can order their own materials. To place your order, call toll-free or visit:

1-866-767-3155

LighthouseCatholicMedia.org/HAPP

3. Have Product Codes Ready

The materials mentioned on the previous page come in packets or kits. *The Retreat Coordinators get the kits; the Retreat Participants get the packets.* There are four product codes to choose from for the retreat materials. Have them handy when you order:

PARTICIPANT PACKET (*with* retreat book) = **LH_PTPKWB**

PARTICIPANT PACKET (*without* retreat book*) = **LH_PTPK**

COORDINATOR KIT (*with* retreat book) = **LH_COKTWB**

COORDINATOR KIT (*without* retreat book*) = **LH_COKT**

---

* If you already have the retreat book, *33 Days to Morning Glory: A Do-It Yourself Retreat in Preparation for Marian Consecration*, you can order your packet or kit without it.

The Participant Packet
and Coordinator Kit

Participant Packet*

PARTICIPANT PACKET INCLUDES:

- *33 Days to Morning Glory Retreat Companion*
- Prayer Card with Consecration Prayer
- *Collection of Daily Prayers*, a greeting-card-sized compilation of the daily prayers for each week.
- Rosary (colors will vary)
- Pamphlet on How to Pray the Rosary
- Miraculous Medal
- 8 ½ x 11 full-color Consecration Day Certificate

COORDINATOR KIT INCLUDES:

- 33 Days to Morning Glory Participant Packet

  - *33 Days to Morning Glory Retreat Companion*

  - Prayer Card with Consecration Prayer

  - *Collection of Daily Prayers*, a greeting-card-sized compilation of the daily prayers for each week.

  - Rosary (colors will vary)

  - Pamphlet on How to Pray the Rosary

  - Miraculous Medal

Coordinator Kit*

  - 8 ½ x 11 full-color Consecration Day Certificate

- *33 Days to Morning Glory: Retreat Talks by Fr. Michael Gaitley, MIC* (DVD set: six sessions, approximately 36 min. each)

- *Retreat Coordinator's Guide*

*Both the Participant Packet and Coordinator Kit are available with or without the Retreat Book, *33 Days to Morning Glory*. (See product code information on oppostie page.) Photos above include the Retreat Book.

Up Next...

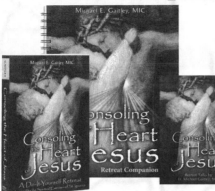

Continue your small-group experience with the next group retreat based on the bestselling book, *Consoling the Heart of Jesus.*

And then...

Complete your faith formation with Stage Two of the Hearts Afire small-group program, which includes *The 'One Thing' Is Three* and the inspirational guide to the works of mercy, *'You Did It to Me.'*

For more information about Hearts Afire Group Retreats, please visit:

LighthouseCatholicMedia.org/HAPP

Hearts **AFIRE**

Parish-based Programs from the
Marian Fathers of the Immaculate Conception